THE
EPISCOPALIAN'S
DICTIONARY

THE
EPISCOPALIAN'S
DICTIONARY

*Church beliefs, terms, customs,
and traditions explained in
layman's language*

HOWARD HARPER

A Crossroad Book   THE SEABURY PRESS ● NEW YORK

The Seabury Press
815 Second Avenue
New York, N.Y. 10017

Copyright © 1974 by The Seabury Press, Inc.
Designed by Carol Basen
Printed in the United States of America

Second printing

LIBRARY OF CONGRESS CATALOGING IN PUBLICATION DATA

Harper, Howard V
   The Episcopalian's dictionary: church beliefs, terms, customs, and traditions explained in layman's language.

   "A Crossroad book."
   1. Protestant Episcopal Church in the U.S.A.—Dictionaries.
I. Title.
BX5007.H37   1975   230'.3'03   74-12105
ISBN 0-8164-1166-2
ISBN 0-8164-2100-5 (pbk.)

To all those hundreds of genial,
devoted, no-nonsense laymen across
this land who tolerated and heartened
me during the fourteen years I had the
joy and the headaches of directing
Laymen's Work, and whom I thought of
then, and still do, as "my boys," this
book is dedicated with appreciation
and affection.

AUTHOR'S
FOREWORD

Laymen have many questions they would like to ask about the Faith and about the Church. I know this from forty years' association with them.

I know also that they have a reluctance about going to the clergy for answers or trying to dig what they want to know out of books. Why is this?

Some insight into this hesitancy may be gathered from the story about the little boy at a picnic who was looking for his mother. He said he wanted to ask her a question. An adult standing by said, "I don't see your mother anywhere around, but there is your father. Why don't you ask him?" "Because," replied the youngster, "I don't want to know that much about it."

Our reverend fathers have the same tendency as other fathers to hand out more information than we can comfortably assimilate.

Another factor in the communication gap between clergy and laity is the language barrier. Every professional discipline develops its own jargon, and its practitioners speak and write in a specialized lingo that is clear to their colleagues but often incomprehensible to others. So laymen give up and let questions go unanswered because experience has taught them that they are likely to come away from a talk with their parson or a session with a religious book more confused than they were before.

There is a third reason for the laymen's reserve, and that is a habit of self-deprecation. When they lack some bit of knowledge, no matter how esoteric the subject may be, they always think it is their own fault. They take for granted that it has been dealt with in their presence—in Church School, in a Confirmation lecture, or in a sermon—but that they must have been looking out the window or daydreaming or dozing at the time, or were just too stupid to grasp and remember what they were told.

I have often puzzled over this inclination on the part of laymen to blame themselves and to be embarrassed over any deficiency in their religious education.

With these facts in mind: (1) that available resources are often verbose, tangential, and boring, (2) that they are frequently couched in obscure terminology, and (3) that there is no disgrace in not possessing all knowledge, I have tried in this book to provide articles and definitions that will be brief but adequate and will be *in the layman's own language.*

Raymond Gram Swing said, "Never underestimate your reader's intelligence, but never overestimate his information." I have made every effort to follow this double injunction.

ABLUTIONS. From the Latin *ablutio:* to wash. The washing of the chalice and paten and the priest's fingers during the service of Holy Communion.

This formal act did not become part of the Eucharist until the tenth or eleventh century, and nowhere is it specifically directed by rubric. All that is officially required is that if any consecrated bread and/or wine remains after the people have received their Communion, "the Minister and other Communicants shall, immediately after the Blessing, reverently eat and drink the same." This is in the rubric at the bottom of page 84 (The Book of Common Prayer), and it really has nothing to do with a ceremonial washing. All it is concerned with is seeing that none of the consecrated bread or wine is carried off and put to some non-religious use, perhaps at some communicant's dinner table.

The washing of fingers and vessels is a more thorough way of taking care that no particle of either consecrated element is left unconsumed. The priest rinses the chalice with wine and drinks it. Then, lest there be a crumb or two adhering to the fingers with which he has handled the bread while consecrating or administering it, he holds those fingers over the chalice and has wine or water, or both, poured over them and drinks it.

It is obvious that this whole procedure is associated with the doctrine of the Real Presence (q.v.). It would be unthinkable to risk having any tiny bit of either element disposed of in some ignoble manner.

The custom now followed almost universally is to take the ablutions just after the last communicant has

1

received instead of waiting until after the blessing. Priests who do this are said to TARP: an acronym formed from the first letters of "Take Ablutions Right Place." And indeed this point in the service is traditionally the right place for them.

It used to be possible to tell a "High Church" priest from a "Low" one by watching where he took the ablutions. The High Churchman TARPed; the Low Churchman waited. Those who TARPed got around their apparent violation of the rubric by pointing out that there was no consecrated bread and wine remaining after the blessing. They had seen to it that there wouldn't be.

ABSOLUTION. From the Latin *ab:* away from, and *solvere:* to loose or set free. The formal act of a priest or bishop pronouncing the forgiveness of the sins of one who has confessed them and is penitent. The power to do this was given to the Apostles by Jesus himself (St. John 20:23) and is passed on to every new priest at his ordination. See Prayer Book, page 546.

Only those churches that are in the Catholic tradition believe that a priest has this authority.

In the Anglican Church confession is publicly made and absolution publicly given in Morning Prayer, Evening Prayer, and the Holy Communion, but this does not mean that we do not practice private confession. Any Anglican priest is ready, and indeed bound, to hear a private confession on request at any time. The difference between the Roman church's position and ours is that with Rome private confession is mandatory while with us it is available but optional.

The Exhortation beginning on page 86 of our American Prayer Book states that one should clear his conscience before receiving the Holy Communion and then goes on to say, "if there be any of you, who

2

by this means cannot quiet his own conscience herein, but requireth further comfort or counsel, let him come to me, or to some other Minister of God's Word, and open his grief; that he may receive such godly counsel and advice, as may tend to the quieting of his conscience, and the removing of all scruple and doubtfulness."

This could be interpreted as merely an offer of pastoral counselling. The English Prayer Book states the Anglican position much more clearly. In the Exhortation from which ours was derived the English say, "let him come . . . . and open his grief, that by the ministry of God's holy Word he may receive the benefit of absolution . . . ."

If that doesn't mean private confession it doesn't mean anything.

ACOLYTE. From the Greek *akolouthos:* an attendant. We use the term to designate the boys (or men) who assist the priest at the altar. We are wrong both historically and semantically. We should call them altar boys or servers, but not acolytes.

An acolyte is an ordained clergyman in the highest of the four minor orders of the Roman Catholic ministry. (The others, in descending importance, are exorcist, reader, and porter.) They are all ordained by the bishop for their respective specific responsibilities.

The duties of an acolyte are just about what we see our servers doing at the altar: lighting and extinguishing the candles and helping the priest generally as he proceeds with the service. But the point is that our boys are not ordained and therefore, if you want to be a purist about it, can't be acolytes in the formal sense. It is really not much of a point. Most of the boys serving at Roman altars nowadays are not ordained either, but they are still called acolytes. Not much is made of the minor orders anymore. The functions are still

3

there, but the ordinations are pretty much omitted.

All boys and men who have been trained as servers should know that you do not have to be in vestments to assist at the altar. If you find yourself at a service where the altar boy has failed to show up, go on up to the altar in your street clothes and give the priest the help he needs.

ADMINISTRATION. This word has, of course, other meanings, but it is always used in connection with the delivery of the bread and wine of the Holy Communion to the people by the priest and/or his assistants. See ADMINISTRATION, SENTENCES OF.

ADMINISTRATION, SENTENCES OF. The words spoken by the priest as he gives the bread and wine to the communicants at the Holy Communion. (Note: a deacon or a layreader may administer the wine.) With each of the elements there are two complete sentences. In the Prayer Book of 1549 only the first sentence was used in each case: "The body of our Lord Jesus Christ . . ." and "The blood of our Lord Jesus Christ. . . ." In 1552 this sentence was dropped and what is now the second one: "Take and eat this . . ." "Drink this . . ." was substituted for it. The Calvinist reformers in England were afraid of any wording that even implied belief in Transubstantiation (q.v.).

In the revision of 1559 the original sentence was restored and the newer one was retained and the two have been used together ever since.

Note that this is the one place in the Eucharist where the second person singular is used: "given for *thee*," "shed for *thee*."

ADVENT. From the Latin *adventus*: coming. The

first season of the Christian year. It begins on the Sunday nearest November 30, which is always the fourth Sunday before Christmas. November 30 happens to be St. Andrew's Day, but this is not as important in connection with Advent as it is made to appear by those who insist on saying that Advent begins on the Sunday nearest St. Andrew's Day. It does, but Advent's relationship is to Christmas, not to St. Andrew's Day.

The penitential nature of Advent as a season of preparation for Christmas is now largely ignored. The newspaper writer who naively said Advent is the Christmas shopping season was only reporting what he saw. There was a time when Advent was marked by some austerity and self-denial, but that is all gone now.

Beginning the day after Thanksgiving, if the storekeepers can wait that long, the air is so full of Christmas carols (mood music to warm the heart and open the purse) that when the Twelve Days of Christmas finally do start most people feel that Christmas is past.

To be fair about it, though, history shows that this time of year has been a time of rejoicing, not penitence. As far back as the records go, and probably before that, people have tended to be joyful about the winter solstice, and the Christian introduction of Advent never really overcame that natural tendency.

The first Advent was set up by the Council of Tours in 567. It was a forty-day pre-Christmas season, running from St. Martin's Day (November 11) to Christmas Eve. In the ninth century it was reduced to its present four-week length. It was a serious time, much like Lent; in fact, it was often called "Winter Lent." No marriages were allowed, fasting and special devotions were ordered, the organ was silenced until the Third Sunday.

Advent has a triple meaning. We are to prepare ourselves for (1) the commemoration of Our Lord's coming into the world on Christmas Day, (2) for his continual coming into our hearts if we will receive him, and (3) for his "second Coming" in glory to judge the world.

AGAPE. A Greek word meaning "love," coined in the early days of Christianity because the other Greek words for love failed to express precisely the new kind of emotion the Christians showed toward one another.

Until Christianity came along, the Greeks could talk about the erotic relationship that exists between men and women or the devotion parents and children have for each other, but they had no word for this new attitude of creative good will the Christians had introduced into community life. So they invented "agape."

In a narrower, specialized sense the new word was applied to the common meal, the "love feast," the early Church held in connection with the weekly celebration of the Holy Communion. It was not long, unfortunately, before abuses that were not far from sacrilege began to creep into this weekly event. In some instances it became a pretty rowdy occasion. Look at I Corinthians 11: 17–34 to see how St. Paul scolds one congregation about what they were making of it.

In an attempt at reform, the Agape was separated from the Holy Communion, with the sacrament being celebrated in the morning and the feast held in the evening. As the gap between Eucharist and Agape widened, the feast gradually lost its original meaning and finally amounted to little more than a charity supper provided for the needy brethren. Eventually it disappeared altogether.

AGNUS DEI. These are Latin words. *Agnus* means "lamb"; *Dei* means "of God."

6

Isaiah 53: 7 refers to the faithful Servant of God as "a lamb that is led to the slaughter," and St. John the Baptist (John 1: 29) says of Jesus, "Behold the Lamb of God, that taketh away the sin of the world." Because of these two scriptural passages Jesus is called "the Lamb of God."

The term *Agnus Dei* is used as the title of a three-part litany that is frequently said or sung in the Holy Communion service, as follows:

> O Lamb of God, that takest away the sins of the world,
> Have mercy upon us.
> O Lamb of God, that takest away the sins of the world,
> Have mercy upon us.
> O Lamb of God, that takest away the sins of the world,
> Grant us thy peace.

When used in the service, the *Agnus Dei* follows the Prayer of Humble Access, Prayer Book, page 82. The rubric permitting (not requiring) a hymn at this point was introduced at the time of the 1928 revision of the Prayer Book. Many parishes were already using it, and the revisers simply recognized the fact that the practice existed and made it legal.

ALB. See under VESTMENTS.

ALLELUIA. A Hebrew phrase meaning "praise Yahweh," lifted directly out of Hebrew without translation and included in many of our hymns and anthems.

ALMS. Money given to the poor or to the Church for the poor. Improbable as it may seem, the word comes by a long and tricky evolution through Latin, Old English, Middle English, and two forms of German, from the Greek word *eleos,* which means "pity."

In earlier times, when the operating budget of the

7

Church was provided by tithes, endowments, and private subsidies, the only money given in the plate at public services was money for the poor—alms. It was offered at the altar and then used by the Church to support such charitable institutions as hospitals, orphanages, homes for the aged, etc. Some alms, of course, went directly to needy individuals or families, through the hands of the priest.

We have come a long way from those uncomplicated times. The word "alms" is archaic now, almost obsolete. Organized charities and government welfare take care of the people who used to depend on alms. And what you put in the plate in church today goes for the budgeted expenses of your parish, your diocese, the national church, and a whole list of other purposes.

The second rubric on page 73 of the Prayer Book says that the "Deacons, Church-wardens, or other fit persons ... shall receive the Alms for the Poor, and other Offerings of the People." Offerings for all purposes are received at the same time and allocated later.

But not much now goes to the poor. The closest thing we have to alms these days is the Rector's Discretionary Fund, which is prescribed by national Canon. Title III, Canon 20 directs that at one service of Holy Communion each month the undesignated offering, which means the loose money not in any kind of envelope, shall be given to the rector to be used among the poor.

And that's all that is left of "the alms" in the Episcopal Church.

ALMS BASIN. The basket, bowl, or plate in which the offering is received at the altar. This receptacle may be made of various materials: rattan, wood, brass, silver, or even gold. The Prayer Book (second rubric on page 73) specifies only that it be "a decent basin."

ALTAR. From the Latin *altare*: a place for burning, which in turn comes from the earlier Latin *adolere*: to burn up.

Literally, an altar is a structure on which sacrificial offerings of animals or incense are burned. It might be a pile of earth or rocks, with a firepan at the top, or it might be an elaborate block of carved stone. However elegant any altar may be today, its origin was in the primitive times when men burned their prize animals to appease the gods.

It has been argued that Christianity has no reason for altars, since Christians have no sacrificial system, at least not of the sort that requires the sacrifice to be consumed by fire. Those who take this position have a point. The sacrifice made by Jesus on Calvary was "once offered" and was "full, perfect, and sufficient . . . for the sins of the whole world." After that, burnt offerings were no longer necessary or appropriate.

When the early Christians met for worship, their emphasis was on the meal they were having, with one another and with their Lord. The Holy Communion was their focal point. And for a meal you need a table, not an altar. Their central piece of furniture was, as St. Paul says, "the table of the Lord" (I Corinthians 10: 21).

At the time of the Reformation in England the word "altar" was dropped from general usage and "table" was substituted for it. In the churches, tables with legs replaced the traditional altars. The Prayer Book still says either "Holy Table" or "Lord's Table"—with one exception: the rubric on page 573, in the Office of Institution of Ministers, directs the newly instituted minister to "kneel before the altar."

9

AMBULATORY. From the Latin *ambulare*: to walk, to go about.

When a church has an apse (q.v.), the contour of the sanctuary is such that the altar necessarily stands out some distance from the wall behind it. Thus, with an apsidal sanctuary, you get a walking space to the rear of the altar. This walk-way is called an ambulatory.

All ambulatories run from one side of the chancel to the other, passing behind the altar as they go. It was only natural, man's desire for embellishment being what it is, that architects should elaborate on this space. In some cathedrals and other large churches the ambulatory has been made into a cloister, closed in by arches, which give the impression of separating it from the sanctuary it surrounds.

Smaller churches seldom do anything fancy with it, and in most cases its only effect is that it allows the altar rail to encircle the altar instead of merely running across from wall to wall in front as it does in square-ended churches.

AMEN. A Hebrew word, brought without change into English. It means "so be it."

From the time of Moses "Amen" was the people's sign of acceptance or ratification of, for example, laws or regulations. After a while the custom arose of saying Amen after the benediction in the synagogue. From there it extended to all prayers.

For the first Christians, who were all Jews, it was second nature to say Amen at the end of a prayer. That they did so is shown in I Corinthians 14: 8–16, in which St. Paul urges ministers to speak distinctly so those who hear him may say Amen with a clear understanding of what they are endorsing. Beginning about the third century, every communicant said Amen to the words with which the bread and wine in Holy Communion were administered to him. It is a pity this

Amen has not been retained in the Prayer Book; but many people are saying it on their own, anyway.

Episcopalians say ah-men; most other communions say aye-men.

In the Book of Common Prayer the word Amen is printed sometimes in italics, sometimes in the same typeface as the text preceding it. If it is in italics it is to be said by the congregation only; otherwise by both minister and people.

AMICE.   See under VESTMENTS.

ANGEL.   From the Greek *angelos*: messenger. "Angel" is the overall word for nine categories of created spirits, superior to man in intellect and will, and whose creation antedates man's. It is also the specific name for the lowest of the nine categories.

The early Christian Fathers grouped angels into the following hierarchy:

Seraphim	Powers
Cherubim	Principalities
Thrones	Archangels
Dominions	Angels
Virtues	

Most of these, except for the cherubim and seraphim, are listed in Ephesians 1: 21 and Colossians 1: 16. The seraphs and cherubs ("im" is simply the Hebrew way of forming the plural of a word) are found in the Old Testament and the Apocrypha.

Some angels have one function, some another. Altogether their jobs add up to five, as follows:

> to praise God and attend upon his throne
> to execute his commands on earth
> to protect the faithful
> to punish the wicked
> to drive away evil spirits

All these duties are stated at one place or another in the Old Testament and the Apocrypha.

Seven archangels are listed by name: Michael and Gabriel in the Old and New Testaments; Raphael, Uriel, Chanuel, Jophiel, and Zadkiel in the Apocrypha.

Milton, in his *Paradise Lost,* gives a roster of those angels who rose in rebellion against Heaven and were exiled. They are known as fallen angels. Satan, or Lucifer, a former archangel, is their chief.

Judaism, Christianity, Islam, and some other Middle Eastern religions all have their angelologies, but in none of them is belief in angels regarded as necessary to salvation.

ANGLICAN COMMUNION, THE. The Church of England plus twenty autonomous, and more or less national, churches that are in communion with the See of Canterbury, which is another way of saying the Church of England. They are, by their official titles:

> The Church of Ireland
> The Church in Wales
> The Episcopal Church in Scotland
> The Protestant Episcopal Church in the United States of America
> The Church in the Province of Burma
> The Anglican Church of Canada
> The Church in the Province of the West Indies
> The Church of England in Australia
> The Church of the Province of New Zealand
> The Church of the Province of Central Africa
> The Church of the Province of South Africa
> The Church of the Province of Kenya
> The Church of the Province of West Africa
> The Church in the Province of Tanzania

The Church of Ugunda, Rwanda, Burundi, and
 Boga-Zaire
The Church in the Province of the Indian
 Ocean
The Nippon Seikokai (Japan)
The Chung Hua Sheng Kung Hui (China)
Igreja Episcopal do Brasil
The Archbishopric in Jerusalem

ANTE-COMMUNION. The first part of the Holy
Communion service down to and including the Gospel. (The English take it on through the Prayer for the
whole state of Christ's Church.)

The first General Rubric, on page 84 of the Prayer
Book, provides that a deacon may say this portion of
the service in the absence of a priest.

In Colonial America the entire Eucharist was said
only four times a year. The customary Sunday morning service consisted of Morning Prayer, the Litany,
and the Ante-Communion, with sermon.

ANTIPHON. From the Greek *anti*: against, and
phone: sound. To sound against. Literally, an antiphon is a song sung back and forth by two choirs, or
by one choir divided into two sections. The word "anthem" comes from the same roots.

In the two-choir sense you won't hear many an-
tiphons in the Episcopal Church. More loosely the
word can be applied to many of the verses and re-
sponses in our services. The Kyrie and the Sursum
Corda are examples. The familiar exchange "The
Lord be with you"—"And with thy spirit" is an antiphon.

APOSTLE. From The Greek *apostolos*—a person
sent, a messenger.

The term is usually understood as being reserved to

those twelve of his followers whom Jesus admitted to an inner, more intimate fellowship with him within the larger company of the disciples. St. Luke 6: 13 says, "He called unto him his disciples: and of them he chose twelve, whom also he named apostles."

Lists of their names are given in St. Matthew 10: 2–4, St. Mark 3: 16–19, St. Luke 6: 14–16, and Acts 1: 13. The lists don't quite tally, and scholars can only guess at the reason for the discrepancies.

Apparently the number twelve was important. After the Ascension St. Peter made a speech declaring that the place of the traitor Judas must be filled in order that the number might be kept at twelve. See Acts 1: 15–26. Perhaps this was because Israel had twelve tribes and it was thought that in the coming Kingdom an Apostle would preside over each tribe. In the same speech St. Peter seemed to rule that only a person who had been with the Lord from his baptism to his ascension was eligible for the position. The Apostles and probably the other disciples present thereupon chose Matthias to fill the vacancy.

However, St. Paul also claimed to be an Apostle, "as one born out of due time," and although there was some disagreement about it at the time, his claim has been generally accepted. He is called "the Apostle Paul" or "Paul the Apostle" throughout Christian literature. Paul himself refers to James, the Lord's brother, as an Apostle (Galatians 1: 19), and St. Luke, in Acts 14: 4, speaks of Barnabas as an Apostle.

While the exact number of those designated as Apostles is open to question, the title was not passed on to future generations of Church leaders, indicating that it implied a direct commission from the Lord.

APOSTLES' CREED. Printed in full on pages 17, 29, 284, and 577 of the Prayer Book, this creed is the oldest universally accepted formal statement of the articles of the Christian faith.

It is an elaboration of some of the baptismal affirmations that had been in use in local parishes in the Western Church in the third and fourth centuries. It was put in its present form in France sometime in the sixth or perhaps the seventh century. It has never been recognized by the Eastern Church. The East uses the Nicene Creed, but its form varies from ours in one detail: they say the Holy Ghost proceeds from the Father *through* the Son, whereas we say he proceeds from the Father *and* the Son.

It was called the Apostles' Creed because it falls into twelve parts, and someone who observed this started the legend that each Apostle had contributed one section, which is, of course, pure fantasy. Both the creed's date and its theological sophistication refute it.

APOSTOLIC SUCCESSION. The doctrine that bishops are the direct inheritors, in an unbroken line, of the ministry to which Jesus himself ordained the Apostles.

St. John 20: 21–23 reads as follows: "Then said Jesus to them again, Peace be unto you: as my Father hath sent me, even so send I you. And when he had said this he breathed on them, and saith unto them, Receive ye the Holy Ghost: whosesoever sins ye remit, they are remitted unto them; and whosesoever sins ye retain, they are retained." There it all is: Christianity's first ordination—the commission and the power to carry on Christ's ministry.

It is this ministry, with its accompanying power, that has been handed down from one bishop to another through all the centuries—so says the doctrine of the Apostolic Succession.

It would be impossible to document this claim with papers that would certify the consecration of every bishop from the Apostles right down to your own bishop. The records are very shaky in some cases and totally missing in others. But the Church has always taken this succession very seriously, and we may be sure that in every consecration of a bishop all through the ages the intention of protecting the source of the new bishop's authority and power was uppermost in the minds of those doing the consecrating, no matter how careful or how careless they may have been about keeping the minutes of the occasion.

Since the Protestant Reformation there have arisen Christian bodies that see no point in maintaining the apostolic ministry. We Anglicans, however, think it is of major importance. We go so far as to name the Historic Ministry as one of the four essentials for the unity of the Christian Church. See LAMBETH QUADRILATERAL.

APSE. From the Greek *apsis*: a fastening together.

In the vocabulary of architecture an apse is a projection added to a building. In church architecture it is the semi-circular or polygonal east end of the building—"east" is where the altar is, no matter what the compass says. And actually, if you stand outside the church and look at the apse it does not take much imagination to see it as an extra section "fastened" onto the main structure.

Not many Anglican churches have apses. There is no particular reason why we should not have them, and some of our especially large churches do have apses. But mostly the churches of the Anglican Communion have been built with square east ends.

ARCHBISHOP. A bishop who, besides having the usual jurisdiction over his own diocese, also has certain administrative and disciplinary authority over the other bishops in a geographical area called a province. His superiority over the other bishops is only a matter of organizational rank. He is no more a bishop than any of his colleagues. He is, as the saying goes, "first among equals."

In most of the twenty-one churches of the Anglican Communion the head bishop (the primate, q.v.) is an archbishop. We Americans call our primate the Presiding Bishop. The Presiding Bishop is, however, an archbishop in everything but title, and there is logical support for those who want to give him the title.

In writing to or speaking of an archbishop the form of address is "The Most Reverend." In speaking to him directly you call him "Your Grace."

See *Presiding Bishop* under BISHOP.

ARCHDEACON. We Anglicans are the only church in which the title of archdeacon is presently anything more than nominal. Not all our dioceses have archdeacons, but in those that do he is given administrative authority over the missions of the diocese, that is, the congregations that depend on diocesan financial aid. Some dioceses divide the responsibility geographically and have more than one archdeacon.

The office started simply enough. It first appears in the fourth century, when the archdeacon was no more than the chief deacon at a cathedral. His first duty was to supervise the other deacons in their work. He was the boss deacon.

But he also had another duty, which in time put him in a position where if he were any kind of politician at all he could make himself the most powerful man in the diocese. He had charge of the distribution of alms. Now, a cathedral is the diocesan church, and a shrewd archdeacon could soon be managing the entire diocesan income. It is axiomatic that the man who holds the purse strings runs the show. If anyone needed any help or favors, the archdeacon, not the bishop, was the man to see. He could give or he could withhold.

One thing led to another, and eventually the archdeacon was top administrative assistant to the bishop. He had crept into this spot by his own devices; there was no canonical provision for it. He became so strong that if the bishop died he took over and ran the diocese until a new bishop was appointed.

A man with such power as this has few friends and many enemies. Naturally there came a time—it was in the thirteenth century—when hostility toward the office of archdeacon reached a point of real rebellion. But the question of how to get rid of him was not an easy one.

His power rested entirely on tradition, not on any canon law. Canons can be changed or revoked, but tradition presents no front against which to make a direct attack. The bishops cleverly got around the problem by creating new offices, such as that of auxiliary bishop, and dividing the archdeacon's work among an enlarged staff. This strategy eventually shrank the archdeacon's duties to almost nothing, and his title became largely an honorary one.

An archdeacon is addressed as "The Venerable" rather than as "The Reverend." Venerable comes from the Latin *venerari*—"to venerate," and *abilis* —"able." It means "worthy to be venerated." There were many centuries when a majority of the clergy did not consider the title appropriate.

The archdeacon system works very well in our democratic American organization. If any diocesan official tries to do any power-grabbing it is hardly ever an archdeacon. We are protected against all over-ambitious climbers by Executive Councils, Standing

Committees, and Diocesan Conventions, none of which were available to the medieval church.

ARTICLE. From the Latin *articulus*: a division or a part. This word has several definitions in the dictionary, one of which is "a particular item of a series in a written document." This is what the Church means by an "article."

For example, in the service of Holy Baptism the person being baptized is asked if he believes "all the Articles of the Christian Faith, as contained in the Apostles' Creed," that is, does he believe all the items in this document?

The word also appears in the title of the set of doctrinal statements beginning on page 603 of the Prayer Book, which are officially called the Articles of Religion but more popularly known as the Thirty-nine Articles.

See THIRTY-NINE ARTICLES, THE.

ARTICLES OF RELIGION. See THIRTY-NINE ARTICLES, THE.

ASCENSION DAY. The festival commemorating the withdrawal of Jesus into Heaven forty days after his resurrection. The account of the event is given by St. Luke in the first chapter of the Acts of the Apostles. Jesus had spent the forty post-resurrection days with his Apostles "speaking of the things pertaining to the Kingdom of God." Now he left them. "He was taken up and a cloud received him out of their sight."

Because it comes forty days after Easter, Ascension Day is always a Thursday.

Some have believed that Ascension Day is the most ancient of all Christian festivals. St. Augustine said

19

the Apostles observed it. He was probably wrong. There is much better evidence that it began in Jerusalem in the late fourth century.

The site of the Ascension, according to St. Luke, was the Mount of Olives, a hill outside Jerusalem. St. Luke says it was "a sabbath day's journey" from the city, which means it was within walking distance—no riding was allowed on the sabbath. If the forty-day calculation is right and this really was a Thursday and not a sabbath, St. Luke must have put that in just to show how far it was.

ASH WEDNESDAY. The first day of the forty-day season of Lent, which ends on the day before Easter. Actually, Ash Wednesday is forty-six days before Easter, but the Sundays in Lent don't count.

The day gets its name from the old custom of marking the forehead with ashes on this day as a sign of penitence. Ashes have always been a symbol of mourning, grief, humiliation, and repentance. Old Testment Jews used to wrap themselves in sackcloth and sit in ashes to show how miserable they were over their sins or their misfortunes.

In all Roman Catholic churches and many of Episcopal churches the faithful go on Ash Wednesday to the altar to have the priest mark their brows with a small smudge of ashes. As he does so he says to each one: "Remember, O man, that thou are dust, and unto dust thou shalt return."

Those who engage in this ceremony regard it as an appropriate way to begin the year's most solemn and longest pentitential season.

ATHANASIAN CREED. This is a long (forty verses), complicated statement that concerns itself mainly with orthodox teaching about the Holy Trinity. It is printed in the English Book of Common Prayer, where it takes up more than two full pages. The accompanying rubric requires that it be said or sung at Morning Prayer on Christmas, Epiphany, Easter, Ascension Day, Whitsunday, Trinity Sunday, and several saints' days.

It is named the Athanasian Creed because originally its authorship was attributed to St. Athanasius, a prominent fourth-century defender of orthodoxy. It was more likely written in France in the fifth century.

There are several reasons why this creed is not used in the Episcopal church. It is long and tedious; parts of it are practically incomprehensible to anyone who has not had theological training; and everything essential in it is already covered in the other two creeds anyway.

AUMBRY. From the Latin *armarium*: a chest. A cupboard in the wall of a church or sacristy where the Reserved Sacrament (q.v.) is kept.

BANNS. From the Middle English *ban*: a proclamation. A public announcement of an intended marriage, made in church during a service.

The custom of publishing banns began in France in the ninth century. From there it spread to England but did not become a requirement until 1200, when the Synod of Westminster declared that no marriage was valid unless banns had been published three times. Fifteen years later Pope Innocent made banns mandatory for the whole Church.

The last rubric on page 304 of the Prayer Book prescribes the exact form in which the banns are to be worded. Their purpose appears here to be solely to give anyone who is aware of an impediment to the marriage an opportunity to make it known, and indeed this was the original reason for banns.

A secondary, and almost equally important, reason was to strike a blow at secret marriages, which abounded in medieval times and were an irritating legal problem. Since such marriages were unrecorded and therefore could not be proved, they endangered the rights of inheritance and they left the legitimacy of children open to question.

With secret marriages in mind, the Council of Trent (1545-1563) tightened up severely on banns. The Council said no marriage existed unless banns were published in the place of residence of both parties on three consecutive Sundays or Holy Days of Obligation. By specifying such days the Council made sure the announcements would be heard by full congregations.

There was a time within the fairly recent past when some states in this country would accept the publishing of banns in lieu of a marriage license. This was still worth noting when the present Prayer Book was revised, in 1928—see the next to last rubric on page 304. There are no states left that give this option now, but you will still hear banns published once in a while, just, apparently, for old times' sake.

BAPTISM. From the Greek *baptizein:* to wash. The sacrament by which a person is initiated into the Christian Church.

The ceremony consists essentially of
(1) promises made by the godparents (q.v.), who represent both the child being baptized and the congregation receiving him, and

(2) the application of water to the head, or sometimes the entire body of the child.

The third rubric on page 273 of the Prayer Book indicates that unless the minister appoints some other time the Baptism is normally held during a service of public worship.

Originally the candidate, adult or child, was totally immersed in the water except in cases where there was a shortage of water or where a complete submerging might be dangerous to his health. Affusion, the pouring of water over the head, was permitted as an alternative. Now affusion is the norm in the Episcopal Church and immersion is practiced only at the request of the candidate or his sponsors.

The Prayer Book, page 292, says Baptism is one of the two sacraments "generally necessary to salvation." (The other is "the Supper of the Lord," that is, the Holy Communion.) To those who think "salvation" means rescue from the fires of hell this dogma, not limited to Anglicans, has caused considerable consternation over the centuries. Calvinists, for example, were devastated by the thought of unbaptized babies suffering eternal torment.

Certainly no mature view of Baptism sees it as a magic trick that saves one from hell by putting a little water on his head. What is really going on at a Baptism is a double action:

(1) The infant is being cleansed of Original Sin (q.v.).

(2) The congregation, through its own participation and/or that of its representatives, the godparents, is receiving the child as a member of the forgiven and forgiving community and is promising to see to his education and nurture in "the things which a Christian ought to know and believe to his soul's health."

As a sacrament Baptism is not valid unless it is administered "in the name of the Father, and of the Son, and of the Holy Ghost," as commanded by the Lord himself in Matthew 28: 19. One supposes, however, that the congregation's responsibilities would remain the same whether the threefold formula were used or not, and that in either case the child would be taken into the love and care of the Christian community.

In these times the candidate is usually a baby or a child not yet old enough to understand the questions that are asked. On page 277 of the Prayer Book provision is made for the baptism of adults, in which case the candidate answers the questions himself and godparents are dispensed with.

BAPTISTRY. A building, separated from but connected with a church, in which Baptism is administered. Many Roman Catholic churches have them; Anglican churches rarely do.

Apparently the point being made by putting Baptism in a separate building was that you have to be baptised *before* you can be a member of the Church. To the Anglicans it seemed just as logical to put the baptismal font immediately inside the door to the nave as a statement that Baptism is the way one enters the Church.

BENEDICTUS QUI VENIT. Latin for the first words of "Blessed is he that cometh in the name of the Lord." According to Matthew 21: 9 this is what the crowds shouted when Jesus rode into Jerusalem on Palm Sunday. The rest of the quotation is, "Hosanna in the highest."

In most ancient liturgies this complete verse was said or sung immediately after the Sanctus. It was dropped from the English Prayer Book in 1552. It has been restored for optional use in the English and Scot-

tish Prayer Books but not in ours. Many of our clergy
put it into the service anyway.

BETROTHAL. From two Middle English words:
be, meaning "in relation to," and *trouthe,* which in its
modern form is our word "truth." "Betroth" therefore
means, literally, "in relation to truth." In church we
use the word "betrothal" to designate the formal and
public exchange of vows, or truths, between two persons who intend to be married.

In earlier times the betrothal took place outside the
church door, on the steps, in the presence of a number
of witnesses, perhaps the whole village. The prospec-
tive bride and groom, before the priest and in the presence of their friends and neighbors, pledged themselves each to the other, gave each other a ring, and
sealed the engagement with a kiss. Peasants and other
poor people who could not afford rings often broke a
coin in two and each party kept one of the pieces.

Included in the ceremony was the bride's father's
public commitment of the woman to this particular
man. This prevented the father from breaking the engagement if some new suitor with a better deal
showed up before the wedding. The arrangement
could be terminated only by mutual consent of the
contracting parties.

There is no real reason for a betrothal ceremony
nowadays but the Church retains a vestige of it at the
beginning of the marriage service itself. See Prayer
Book, pages 300 and 301. The congregation, representing the public in general, are given an opportunity
to say so if they know of any impediment to the marriage; the bride and groom are charged to reveal any
obstacle that either of them may know. The service
then goes on to the betrothal vows (not the marriage
vows) in which both questions and answers are in the

future tense—"Wilt thou . . . ?" and "I will," recalling the times when all this was done weeks or months before the wedding.

After these preliminary vows the bride's father "gives her away." It should be noted that he places her hand in the clergyman's hand, not the groom's. The symbolism here is that the father gives her to the Church and the Church gives her to the groom.

Up to this point everything takes place at the chancel steps. It is only after the betrothal that the wedding party, minus the bride's father, moves up to the altar rail and the actual marriage service begins.

BIER. The frame or stand on which the coffin is placed in the church prior to and during the Order for the Burial of the Dead.

BIRETTA. A cap, so called from the Old Provençal *berret,* the same word from which we get "beret."

It probably started as a soft cap much like the modern beret but has long since evolved into a stiff, brimless, four-cornered hat with three upright projections and a pompon on top. (Bishops' birettas have four projections.) It is worn by most Roman clergy and some Anglicans.

Priests wear black birettas, bishops purple ones, cardinals red ones. Some Anglican deans and canons affect purple pompons.

The biretta is always lifted when the name of Jesus is spoken.

BISHOP. A member of the highest of the three orders of ministers in the Christian Church. The Latin word for bishop is *episcopus.* "Bishop" is not a translation of it; it is just what English has done to it.

Only bishops have a power to ordain. It takes three bishops to ordain ("consecrate" is the more common term) another bishop. This is a safety measure. It started in the days when one could not always be sure that any given bishop had been properly consecrated. The Church felt that if you have three, the orders of one of them are pretty sure to be valid.

In our American church there are four kinds of bishops: Presiding, Diocesan, Coadjutor, and Suffragan. No one kind is any more a bishop than the others—the differences are in their functions and duties.

(1) *Presiding Bishop.* The chief bishop of our church, elected by the House of Bishops for a term ending at the General Convention nearest his sixty-eighth birthday. His election is subject to the approval or veto of the House of Deputies, though the Deputies have no part in electing him. Because both Houses are involved, the election always takes place at a General Convention, which is the only time the House of Deputies is in session. On assuming office the Presiding Bishop gives up his diocese and goes to live in Dover House, near Greenwich, Connecticut. His office is in New York City. He has a throne, which is in the Cathedral of St. Peter and St. Paul in Washington, D.C., because he has no cathedral of his own. His duties are almost entirely administrative. He presides over the House of Bishops and over the quarterly meetings of the Executive Council; he does a formidable amount of traveling and speech-making; he holds a great many *ex officio* positions that require attendance at various committee and board meetings; and he snatches what time he can to try to cope with the mountains of mail he gets. He has the toughest job in the church, and he would probably tell you it can be the most rewarding.

(2) *Diocesan Bishop.* The chief pastor of one diocese. He is elected by a Convention of the diocese of which he is to be the head. His election must be ap-

proved by a majority of the dioceses of the church, since after all, though his responsibilities will be in one diocese, he is nevertheless a bishop of the whole Church. His duties are to visit his parishes for Confirmation and other occasions, to be a pastor to his clergy, to preside over meetings of his Executive Council and his Diocesan Convention, and to look after administrative matters generally. He also spends a lot of time trouble-shooting and worrying about money, but these activities are not stated in the Canons as part of his episcopal assignment.

(3) *Coadjutor Bishop.* The word comes from the Latin *adjutare:* to help, plus *con:* with. A Coadjutor Bishop is a helper to the Diocesan but his special prerogative is his automatic right of succession when the Diocesan retires or dies. It is customary for the Diocesan to assign an area of the diocese to the Coadjutor as his own responsibility.

(4) *Suffragan Bishop.* Suffragan comes from the Latin *suffragari,* which means to support with one's vote. We get "suffrage" from the same root. It would be pretty tactless of a Suffragan Bishop not to vote along with the Diocesan, though he might get away with it if the ballot were a secret one. The Suffragan is an assistant to the Diocesan but does not have the right of succession.

Both Coadjutor and Suffragan Bishops have to go through the same election and approval procedures as the Diocesan does.

BISHOP, TRANSLATION OF. The moving of a bishop from one diocese to another.

It has always been permissible for a Suffragan Bishop or the bishop of a Missionary Diocese to be elected to, and accept, another jurisdiction. The privilege now extends to Diocesan Bishops and Coadjutor Bishops as well.

No bishop can change dioceses until he has served five years in his present one, and his move needs the consents of a majority of the bishops and Standing Committees of the Church.

BOOK OF COMMON PRAYER, THE. The first Prayer Book of Anglicanism, compiled by Thomas Cranmer, Archbishop of Canterbury, appeared in 1549.

Cranmer had several reasons for producing this book. The first, and by far the most important, was to translate the old Latin services into English so that the laity could understand what they heard in church. This he accomplished with a dignity of style and beauty of diction that have never been surpassed, perhaps not even equalled, in all of English literature.

His second, more practical, purpose was to gather into one volume the multiplicity of service books the clergy had to have in order to conduct public worship. The number of such tomes was unbelievable. Each minister had to have a book for his own part in the service. One had the prayers, another the Epistles, another the Gospels, another the Psalms, and so on and on. By Cranmer's time they had managed to get everything for the Mass into one book, the Missal (q.v.), but that did not solve the problem, for there were still the Daily Offices, the Occasional Offices, and many litanies. A clergyman could spend minutes looking for his place when his turn came to get into the act. If one priest was trying to run the service alone, he had to go from one book to another. Cranmer himself said it was harder to find what to read than to read it when it was found.

The early Christians had used no books at all except the Bible. By the sixteenth century there were manuals for everything. Thomas Cranmer got them all together, translated them, and came up with what he said was "a single, convenient guide for priest and people."

These two purposes were not the only ones the Archbishop had in mind. He also felt that his single, convenient guide would help to unify the nation. England had for centuries used the Roman liturgy, but during those centuries many local customs and peculiarities had developed. A man from London going to Mass in York might find the service scarcely recognizable. One book, used by all parishes across the country would, Cranmer believed, bring about a uniformity of worship. And since the Protestant Reformation was now breaking England up into partisan factions—Calvinists, Romanists, traditional Anglicans, etc.—a ceremonial homogeneity might well spill over into the political area.

Cranmer also wanted the laity to be able to join intelligently in the services of the Church. His book gave them things to do and things to say; it made them participants in the act of worship, not mere spectators.

That one sentence of his, quoted above, just about sums it up: his book was a *single* volume, it was a *guide*, and it was for priest and *people*. All you have to add is that it was in English.

There was not much that was new in that 1549 book. It was a translation of material that had been around, most of it, for a long time. Cranmer had a genius for handling the old in a new and graceful way and expressing it magnificently.

Cranmer's personal mood was more Protestant than Catholic. He had spent some time in Germany and had been influenced by the Lutheran theologians there. He thought he was presenting the country with a Protestant Prayer Book. But when it was put into use throughout England on Whitsunday, 1549, nobody, especially the Protestants, liked it much. What he had overlooked was that most of the English Protestants were Calvinists, not Lutherans. The book lasted only until All Saints' day, 1552, when it was replaced by a radical revision engineered mainly by the Calvinists.

In 1553, when Mary (Bloody Mary) came to the throne, the 1552 book was suppressed and the Roman rites, as they had been back in the reign of Henry VIII, were revived.

Elizabeth I followed Mary as Queen. In 1559 she restored the 1552 book, which, with minor changes and additions, remained in use for nearly a century. The Puritans threw it out in 1645, when they were running the country. (Remember, the Church of England is a "state church," which means that Parliament is in charge of ecclesiastical as well as civil affairs.)

It was brought back when the Monarchy was restored in 1660, and with a little revision by Conservatives in 1662, is pretty much the Prayer Book used in England today. It was the only Prayer Book the American Colonies knew.

The first American Prayer Book came out in 1789. It was not greatly different from the English one. Its Preface says "this Church is far from intending to depart from the Church of England in any essential point of doctrine, discipline, or worship; or further than local circumstances require." The sort of thing "local circumstances" required, for example, was that Americans stop praying for the royal family and switch to the President of the United States.

And so it went in this country for a hundred years —the English Prayer Book of 1662 with certain necessary American adjustments. But during those hundred years the United States expanded and changed so much that a seventeenth-century manual of devotions from a rural, agriculturally-oriented island across the ocean didn't fit any more. (It didn't fit England very well any more, either, but that is beside the present point.) These were the times of which Walt Whitman

said, "I hear America singing"—times of industrializa-
tion, growth, and the opening of the West, times of
social upheaval. The American Church had to have a
new Prayer Book, suited to her new conditions and
needs. In 1892 she got one. The changes in the new
book were many and sweeping, but there were men of
influence and vision who felt that they did not go far
enough and the book was revised again in 1928.

And now, once again, we are in the throes of revision fever. The 1964 General Convention approved
the principle of trial use of proposed revisions prepared by the Standing Liturgical Commission. There
followed *The Liturgy of the Lord's Supper* (1967),
Services for Trial Use (1970), and *Authorized Services
1973,* all of which have introduced more variety (and
confusion) into Episcopal parish worship than it has
ever known before. All this could result in a revised
American prayer book in 1979. The same kind of thing
is going on in every province of the Anglican Communion except in the Indian Ocean Province.

Cranmer's Prayer Book of 1549 has not been revised
often in its 425 years of existence. The Church does
not move quickly or capriciously in such matters, but
you may be sure there will always be revisions of the
Prayer Book.

"Our fathers have been Churchmen
Nineteen hundred years or so,
And to every new suggestion
They have always answered No!"

Which is not really a bad thing. New suggestions
if they are any good, always get through in the
end, and the typical Anglican aversion to change very
often keeps the Church from painting itself into a
corner.

BLESSED SACRAMENT. Another of the various terms used for the Holy Communion.

It is also applied to the consecrated elements themselves, that is, the bread and wine.

BURSE. From the Greek *byrsa:* a bag. A pocket or case made of two squares of some rigid material —cardboard, wood, glass—covered with cloth, sometimes in the seasonal color, sometimes plain white regardless of the season. It is one of the furnishings of the altar at the Holy Communion. Its function is to contain the corporal (q.v.).

C

CANDIDATE. A person who has been officially admitted by his bishop to study for Holy Orders.

To attain the status of candidate he has had to go through a long, tedious screening process designed to assure the Church that its clergymen will be healthy, intelligent, and competent. He must have satisified his parish priest, his vestry, his diocesan Commission on the Ministry, the diocesan Standing Committee, and finally his bishop, that his reasons for seeking ordination are worthy ones, that his educational level is adequate, and that his physical and mental health are sound.

Only after all these tests, consultations, and examinations can he qualify as a candidate, and all it means is that he is now allowed to study. It is no guarantee that he will be ordained.

If this seems a severe way of culling out the misfits before they get in, well, it is. But in the end it is a kindness. It protects the Church against unsuitable clergy, but it also protects the man against wasting several years of his life before he finds out he doesn't belong in the ministry.

CANDLES. From the Latin *candeo:* I burn. Nobody needs to be told what a candle is. This is about candles in the Church.

Today they serve no practical purpose. Electricity offers better, quicker, and cheaper illumination. Candles are leftovers from the time when they were the only source of light men had. We continue to use them in church now for much the same reason a hostess uses them on her dinner table: for their soft, warm, unmechanized glow.

In its early centuries the Church had to stay pretty much underground. Christians held their services in dark places: Roman Christians in the catacombs, others in blacked-out houses. They had to have candlelight to see what they were doing.

By the time candles were no longer needed they had become a traditional part of public worship. Ceremonial acts had grown up around lighting them, carrying them, and extinguishing them. They were kept in the ritual, out of habit or nostalgia, and rationalized, as St. Jerome put it, as being there "not to drive away the darkness but as a sign of spiritual joy."

We would miss them if we didn't have them. If you go to church in Ireland, for example, you have a feeling that something is not quite right and after a while you realize that what is troubling you is that there are no candles on the altar.

The Roman Church has used candles without any interruption since early times, but Anglicans did without them for the most part for three centuries or more. When the Puritans got the upper hand in the Church of England they threw them out along with all the other ornaments they considered "Popish." It was not until the Oxford Movement (q.v.) came along in the nineteenth century that Catholic traditions were revived in Anglicanism. Colored stoles, processions, crosses—and candles—began to creep back in, against furious resistance in many instances. Less than a hundred years ago these things and many others that we now take for granted were violently controversial both in England and America.

Now that we have candles back we have them without the meticulously detailed regulations that the Roman Church never gave up, and parishes in the Episcopal Church differ widely in their use of them. Two Eucharistic candles, lighted for the Holy Communion, are fairly general now, but from there on each parish does largely as it pleases. For "office lights" (candles used at all services) some have candelabra; some have a row of single lights. Some have only a few; some pack all they can into the available space. And some add an extra candle when the bishop is present. In Episcopal parishes across the land the intensity of fire on the altars ranges from a glimmer to a conflagration.

Judaism had—and has—its ceremonial lights, both for home and public worship, and they meant—and mean—just about what ours do: a sign of spiritual joy, a symbol of the light of heaven. But it would not be accurate to say we inherited ours from Judaism. If we did it was a long-deferred legacy, for there were centuries between Jewish and Christian ritual candles, centuries during which the Christians' candles had no religious significance at all. They were purely functional; they just gave light to see by.

CANON. From the Greek *kanon:* a rod. In Greek usage the rod came to have the special meaning of "a carpenter's rule," and from there it was a short step to making it mean simply a measure or a standard. We do the same thing with our word "yardstick." We have "yardsticks" by which we determine whether almost anything, from a man's intelligence to a bird-dog's nose, comes up to the required level of excellence.

Canon Law.   This is the collection of ecclesiastical laws that serves as the rules of church government. Examples would be the canon on marriage, the canon on the election of a bishop, the canon on admission to Holy Orders, etc. Each canon tells what you must do or can't do about the subject in question.

The national Church has its canons and the dioceses have theirs, just as the Federal government and the states have their separate laws. In both Church and civil government the principle holds true that the local unit may not make laws that conflict with those of the national body.

Canon of Scripture.   This means the books of the Bible that are accepted by the Church as genuine and inspired. The Roman Church includes the books of the Apocrypha in its canon but the Anglican does not. Instead, we put them in a separate section bound between the Old and New Testaments, for which our explanation is that "the Church doth read (them) for example of life and instruction of manners, but yet doth it not apply them to establish any doctrine." (Articles of Religion, Article VI, Book of Common Prayer, page 604.)

Canon of the Mass.   The Prayer of Consecration of the bread and wine in the service of Holy Communion. This prayer is considered as beginning with the *Sursum corda* ("Lift up your hearts.") on page 76 in the Book of Common Prayer and ending with the Lord's Prayer on page 82.

Major, Minor, and Honorary Canons. These are people, not laws or standards, but here again a legal, or canonical, compliance is involved. These men are called canons only because they are listed on the canonical (official) roster of a cathedral staff.

Major canons are those who, under the direction of the dean, hold certain fixed assignments, and titles to go with them, e.g. the Canon Almoner, whose responsibility it is to distribute the alms of the cathedral or to make suggestions about how they should be distributed; the Canon Sacristan, who looks after the altar and the altar supplies and furnishings, which are kept in the sacristy.

Minor canons are of a lower rank. They have no titles or set responsibilities. They might be compared with curates on the staff of any large parish. Their duties vary according to the dean's immediate needs for their help.

Honorary canons are just what the term suggests. The bishop, wishing to honor some distinguished or especially beloved clergyman in his diocese, to give status to some member of his own staff, or to recognize the achievements of some nationally prominent priest outside the diocese, makes him an honorary canon of the bishop's cathedral. It is something like an honorary doctorate given by a college or university, except that it carries with it two perquisites a college cannot give: a permanent stall in the choir of the cathedral and permanent altar privileges.

CANTERBURY CAP. A soft, flat, square black hat worn only by the Anglican clergy and by no means all of them. Some consider it interchangeable with the biretta (q.v.), but the Canterbury cap is preferred by those who think the biretta is too Romish and yet want to wear something on their heads. The points of the cap are worn at the front, rear, and sides.

CANTERBURY, SEE OF. The number one diocese of the Church of England and, by tradition and general consensus, of the entire Anglican Communion. Located in the county of Kent, fifty-five miles southeast of London, it was founded late in the sixth century by St. Augustine, who was its first archbishop.

Although all the national churches of Anglicanism are autonomous, they retain a traditional connection with Canterbury and look to the Archbishop of Canterbury as nominal head of the Church. He has no legal authority in any of them except the Church of England.

It was in Canterbury Cathedral (right name: the Cathedral Church of Christ) that St. Thomas Becket, then archbishop, was assassinated in 1170. A shrine soon developed at his tomb, which became the principal pilgrimage center of England and continued so until it was destroyed by Henry VIII in 1538. One of these pilgrimages is the setting for Chaucer's Canterbury Tales.

It is interesting that we get our word "canter" from these pilgrimages. The term came to denote the easy trot to which Canterbury pilgrims set their horses.

CANTICLE. From the Latin *canticulum:* a song. In the Church a canticle is a song derived from the Bible, used in liturgical worship.This definition, for some strange reason, excludes the Psalms, which are certainly songs and certainly from the Bible. Many of our canticles, however, are direct excerpts from Psalms.

The canticles we use are on pages 9 to 15 and pages 26 to 29 of the Prayer Book.

CATHEDRAL. The church in which the bishop's throne, or *cathedra,* is kept. *Cathedra* is the Greek word for seat. The cathedral is therefore the bishop's church, the diocesan church, the place where the seat of diocesan authority is located.

Properly, a cathedral does not have any communicants of its own. It is not a parish church; therefore it has no parishioners. That is why you may see chairs instead of pews in a cathedral. Pews used to be owned or rented by families or individuals who were members of the local parish. So pews came to symbolize a membership.

There are few true cathedrals in the Episcopal Church. St. John the Divine, in New York, and Saints Peter and Paul, in Washington, are the examples that come readily to most peoples' minds. Most others are "pro-cathedrals," that is, parish churches used as cathedrals. They are supported, entirely or in part, by their own parishioners.

You may have a bishop's chair in the sanctuary of your parish church. From a literal point of view there could be some question about whether the bishop can have a chair anywhere except in his cathedral. The Roman Church thinks he shouldn't. When he visits a parish they bring a plain chair in for him. His cathedra, they say, is back in the cathedral where it belongs. They may be right.

CATHOLIC. From the Greek *katholikos:* general or universal. In connection with Christianity the word is first met with in the writings of St. Ignatius of Antioch, who died in 117.

Because Christianity is now split up into so many divisions, there is no possibility today of having a church that is Catholic in the original sense of the word. No one church is universal. Some people say the Catholic Church in modern terms means "the great world-wide body of all believers," fragmented as that body is. These are the same people who smilingly say we are all on the same train headed for the same place but in different cars. This is sweet and sentimental, but both theologically and semantically it is palpable nonsense. All those people in all those different cars may be Christians but they are by no means all Catholics.

The closest you can come to a Catholic Church in these times is a church that possesses a historical and continuous tradition of faith and practice and a ministry that is in the Apostolic Succession (q.v.). On those considerations we Anglicans qualify as Catholics, as do the Eastern Orthodox, the Roman Catholics, and some others.

CELEBRANT. The officiating priest at the Holy Communion, as distinguished from any assistants he may have at the altar with him.

CENSER. See THURIBLE.

CHALICE. From the Latin *calix:* cup. The cup used to contain the wine at the Holy Communion.

CHANCEL. From the Latin *cancelli:* a grating or lattice. This is the part of the church interior between the nave and the altar. It contains the choir stalls and the prayer desks for the clergy. It is usually a few steps higher than the nave.

The reason this area is called a lattice is that in earlier times it was frequently screened off from the main body of the church by a more or less ornate partition made of wood or wrought iron which sometimes looked not unlike lattice-work. Literally, then, the chancel is that division of the building that is behind the *cancelli.* Many old churches, particularly in England and on the Continent, still have such screens.

CHANCEL SCREEN. A screen, sometimes of

solid wood, sometimes of wooden or metal openwork, separating the chancel from the nave. If a chancel screen is surmounted by a cross it is called a rood screen and the beam on which the cross stands is a rood beam. The old English word for cross was "rood."

Americans don't see many chancel screens in these times. The currently popular styles of church architecture allow no place for them. But there are still many such screens in England.

CHAPEL. From the Latin *cappella:* a cape. The connection between a cape and what we today think of as a chapel is not readily apparent, but it's there.

The Kings of France, when they were on military campaigns, carried with them the cape of St. Martin as a sacred relic that would help them in battle. The tent or other temporary structure that housed the *cappella* was called a chapel. That is how the word began.

By extension it was soon applied to shrines built to contain other relics.

Now it has many meanings. A few examples are: a small room set aside in a hospital or school for worship and meditation, a church on a college campus, a part of a cathedral or large church with a separate altar.

CHOIR. From the Latin *chorus*: a group of singers. The Latin word also has been carried into English without translation and it doesn't need any. A choir is indeed a group of singers, who assist in services of worship.

Such bodies existed as early as the fourth century, but until about the fifteenth century they were made up of clergy and boys. As church music became more complex, lay singers were admitted, and by the nineteenth century the clergy, except in monasteries, had dropped out and had been replaced by laymen and women, often professionals.

As an architectural term, the choir is the part of the church in which the clergy and the choristers are seated.

CHRISM. From the Greek *chrisma*: an anointing. A mixture of olive oil and balsam, used in Eastern, Roman, and some Episcopal churches. The Roman Church also puts in other perfumes besides balsam.

Chrism is used at Baptism, Confirmation, and Ordination, as well as at the consecration of churches and the blessing of altars, chalices, etc.

Chrism is not the same as other holy oils, such as those used for the unction of the sick, to which no balsam is added.

Both chrism and other holy oils must be blessed by the bishop.

CIBORIUM. A Latin word meaning "cup." A chalice-shaped vessel, with a lid, used to contain the sacramental bread before it is placed on the altar to be consecrated at the Eucharist. It may also be used to contain the Reserved Sacrament (q.v.).

CLERICAL COLLAR. The clergyman's streetwear badge of his office. It is a stiff white collar worn back-to-front by Anglican, Roman, and Lutheran ministers, and increasingly by clergy of other communions.

In America it is commonly known simply as a clerical collar, though occasionally some wag will call it a "backwards" collar. The British, with their compulsion to give everything a cute nickname, call it a "dog collar."

There are two notions about its origin. One takes it all the way back to Roman times and says it was a scarf or kerchief worn by orators to protect the neck and throat from cold and to prevent the top of the toga from being stained by perspiration.

Another explanation is that it is a stylized form of the white neckband, or "stock," which was the fashion for all men from the sixteenth century up into the early eighteen hundreds.

In either case a considerable evolution had to take place.

The development of the collar from the stock seems to have the more plausible historical support. It is said that the conservative leaders of the Oxford Movement, who, in their desire to distinguish the appearance of the clergy from that of the laity, ignored the advent of the modern collar and modified the stock to produce the present clerical collar. This account gives it a religious association the Roman scarf did not have.

The Oxford Movement (q.v.) began in 1833. The clerical collar is therefore only a little more than a century old.

CHRISTEN. From the Latin *christianus*: Christian. To christen someone means to make him a member of the Christian Church. Since the officially prescribed way to do this is through the Sacrament of Holy Baptism, "to christen" has by association become synonymous with "to baptize."

Also, because the person being baptized is given his Christian name at the same ceremony, the word has picked up a further meaning: "to name." This is why people say they are "christening" ships and various other items of military or institutional paraphernalia when what they are actually doing is going through some traditional ritual in which these things are given names. To caricature the Sacrament of Holy Baptism by smashing a bottle of champagne against a warship and saying they had thereby made a Christian of the ship would be sacrilegious if the perpetrators of the caricature knew what they were doing.

CHURCH, THE. From the Greek *kurios*: master or lord. One form, *kuriakon*, of this word meant "something pertaining to, or belonging to, the Lord," and was applied originally to a church building. The Romance languages get their word for church, for example the French *église,* from another Greek word, *ekklesia*, which meant an assembly, primarily an assembly of citizens of a self-governing city.

We use "church" in both senses: the building and the congregation, but when we talk about *the* Church we are talking about something much bigger than either of them. We mean the whole world-wide Christian community, founded by Christ himself and endowed by him with the Holy Spirit at Pentecost.

The Church has four essential characteristics, as it is described in the historic creeds. It is One—a unit; it is Holy—of divine origin; it is Catholic (q.v.); and it is Apostolic, that is, its history is continuous from the time of the Apostles.

Such a body is visible, right there to be seen. No vague "universal company of all believers" meets this specification.

Where, in our time, is this visible body? Rome claims it is in Roman Catholicism; Eastern Orthodoxy claims it is in Eastern Orthodoxy. We Anglicans don't claim it is in Anglicanism. We say it isn't actually anywhere now. Everyone knows the Church Christ founded is split into many pieces. But we do claim we are as close as you can get to that One, Holy, Catholic, and Apostolic Church—as close as Orthodoxy is and as close as Rome is.

The separation of Catholics from Orthodox, of Protestants from Catholics, and of Protestants from one another is not merely an academic squabble among theologians; it is one of the scandals that prevents the Church from being the Church.

Of course, one feels there is some eventual hope in the "Ecumenical Movement" so much talked about these days. This movement thus far is mostly just an indication of a disposition on the part of various Christian groups to work together organizationally in matters of social action and to talk together about the things that keep them apart organically.

So what is the Church? Right now it is the Holy, Catholic, and Apostolic, but fragmented adumbration, mutilated but living, of the community our Lord established. Which means that it isn't really quite the Church at all.

CLOISTER. From the Latin *claudere*: to close. An architectural rather than an ecclesiastical word. A cloister is a covered walk with an open colonnade on one side, running between two buildings or between different parts of the same building.

Such walkways are often seen attached to buildings that have nothing to do with a church, but in earlier times most of them were parts of cathedrals and monasteries and the word acquired a churchly flavor in the popular mind.

By a process of evolution "cloister" came to mean a monastery or a convent, simply because that was where most cloisters were.

Religious orders that do not permit their members to leave the monastery or convent are known as "cloistered" orders.

COADJUTOR BISHOP. See under BISHOP.

COLLECT. From the Latin *collecta*: assembly. Normally we use the word in specific reference to the prayer in the Eucharist that precedes the Epistle and Gospel for the day.

Some scholars will tell you this Collect is so called because it binds together the main thoughts of the Epistle and Gospel. Sometimes it does, but these occasions are rare, and one would be on shaky ground if he claimed that this is always the purpose of the Collect, or if it is, that the Collect always accomplishes it. The Latin derivation of the word shows that it refers to a prayer said before an assembly, or congregation.

A Collect is any short prayer containing (1) an invocation, (2) a petition, and (3) a pleading in Christ's name or an ascription of glory to God.

COLORS. It is customary to say we Episcopalians follow the Roman Catholic system in our use of colors for our vestments and altar hangings and that we do so because the Church of England never had a color system for us to inherit. It is not quite that simple. We do use the Roman colors, but it is not true that there were no English ones we could have used.

The Church in America used no colors at all while it was part of the Church of England (1607–1776) nor for a century after that. Colors had dropped out of English church life at the Reformation.

Before the Reformation there had been so many color schemes in the English Church it almost seemed that every diocese had one of its own. The one at Salisbury Cathedral was regarded more or less as the standard for England, but it was so complicated and required so many sets of vestments that few parishes could afford to imitate it. In the fourteenth century Bishop John Grandison had a plan drawn up for his own diocese (Exeter) that was much like the one we have today, but the similarity was coincidental. It would not be accurate to say we adopted the Exeter system.

After the Reformation altars went bare and clergy wore black until well up into the nineteenth century in England, and of course here in the Colonies. With the Oxford Movement (q.v.) there came a wave of interest in ancient Catholic traditions among some of the English clergy, one result of which was that they introduced seasonal colors into their churches.

It is impossible to be precise about when or where the use of colors came into the American Church. It just seeped in here and there, often amid howls of protest. There was never a time when the clergy all got together and decided that from then on they would put the seasonal colors into their parishes. Nor was there ever a time when everyone agreed to adopt the Roman sequence. Nevertheless, it happened, and what is commonplace to us today was only a hundred years ago a matter of raging controversy. Resistance among the laity was violent.

The colors commonly used, together with their meanings and times appropriate for them, are as follows:

Purple. The color for penitence. Used in Advent and Lent, and sometimes at burials. Worn by priests hearing confessions.

White. The festival color, representing joy and purity. Worn on Christmas, Easter, the great festivals of the Lord (e.g. Ascension Day), days set apart for the Blessed Virgin Mary, days for saints who were not martyred. Also at baptisms and weddings, and sometimes at burials.

Red. The Holy Spirit's color. Worn on Whitsunday (though the name of the day means "white" Sunday). Also at confirmations and ordinations. Being the color of blood, red is used on martyred saints' days.

Green. The color of growing things. In the Epiphany season it signifies the growth and spread of the Church. The rationale here is that the visit of the Wise Men at the first Epiphany symbolized the extension of the Gospel to the Gentile world. In Trinity it stands for the growing verdure of the fields and forests at this time of year.

Black. The mourning color. Worn on Good Friday and at burials.

COMMUNICANT. From the Latin *communicare:* to share or partake. Anyone who is a member of any group is, in the broadest sense of the word, a communicant of that group, because he shares in its common life.

Here, however, we are concerned with what it takes to make one a communicant of the Protestant Episcopal Church in the United States of America. Title I, Canon 16, Section 3, says, ". . . all members in good standing who have been confirmed . . . or have been received into this Church by a Bishop of this Church, and who shall, unless for good cause prevented, have received Holy Communion at least thrice during the next preceding year, are communicants in good standing."

"The next preceding year" is not precisely delineated. The next preceding year from when? It doesn't say. And what is "good cause"? That is not defined either.

Traditionally the times for the three required communions have been Christmastide, Eastertide, and Whitsuntide. But the Canon does not mention this tradition, much less support it. A literal-minded member of the Church could receive his three communions on three successive days at any time during the year and still be a communicant "in good standing" within the terms of the canon.

See under MEMBER.

COMMUNION OF SAINTS, THE. One of the Articles of the Christian Faith to which we commit ourselves when we accept the Apostles' Creed.

It has been held to have two interpretations:

(1) The spiritual union between Christ and each individual Christian, and, by derivation, among all Christians both living and dead.

(2) The fellowship of all Christians on earth only.

The former is traditionally considered the correct view of what the doctrine means.

The word "saints" is used here in its original sense as including all who have been baptized.

See under SAINT.

COMPLINE. See under OFFICE.

CONFESSION. Do Anglican priests hear private confessions? The answer is Yes—at the request of the penitent. If you ask one of our priests to hear you, he is bound by tradition and precedent to listen. The only real difference between Rome and us on this score is that Rome has traditionally required private confession and absolution as a prerequisite to receiving the Holy Communion and we do not.

Read the Exhortation that begins on page 86 of the Prayer Book. Its last paragraph says ". . . if there be any of you, who by this means cannot quiet his own conscience herein, but requireth further comfort or counsel, let him come to me, or to some other Minister of God's Word, and open his grief . . . ." At this point the American Prayer hedges a bit. It goes on: "that he may receive such godly counsel and advice, as may tend to the quieting of his conscience." That sounds as if we want the penitent to confess his sins and then just get a good pep-talk. He would do as well, maybe better, to go to a psychiatrist.

The English Prayer Book, in practically the same Exhortation, beats around no such bush. It comes right out with, "that by the ministry of God's holy Word he may receive absolution." That, presumably, is what he came for.

There is one other reference to private confession in the Prayer Book. It is in the last rubric on page 313: "Then shall the sick person be moved to make a special confession of his sins . . . ."

CONFIRMATION. From two Latin words: *firmare*, which means "to strengthen" and *com*, an intensive, adding extra force to *firmare*. A literal translation would be "to strengthen greatly."

In the Church Confirmation is a ceremony in which the bishop lays his hands on a person's head to complete the strengthening gift of the Holy Spirit that was bestowed on that person at his baptism. The indication that this action is necessary in addition to baptism is seen in Acts 8: 14–17, in which it is told that when St. Peter and St. John found that the brethren in Samaria had received only baptism, "then laid they their hands upon them and they received the Holy Spirit."

In the Prayer Book, page 296, the title of the service makes it clear that Confirmation is for those who have "come to years of discretion." A strict application of this proviso might rule out some individuals no matter how old they were, but the Episcopal Church generally accepts eleven or twelve as the minimum age of eligibility.

The Roman and Eastern churches consider Confirmation a sacrament. So do many Anglicans, but they do so without the official support of their church. Article XXV of the Articles of Religion (Prayer Book, page 607) says it is not to be counted as a "Sacrament of the Gospel."

There is a tendency among us to regard Confirmation as "joining the Church" if the person being confirmed is an adult, or a sort of Bar Mitzvah* if he is a youngster. This may be partly because the person is required to go through a course of instruction prior to his Confirmation and partly because the rubric on page 299 of the Prayer Book does not admit him to the Holy Communion until he is confirmed or ready to be confirmed.

This rubric is widely violated in these days of ecumenicity, which may or may not be a good thing. It was certainly a good thing that the Church in the American Colonies ignored it. From the founding of Jamestown in 1607 until the consecration of Samuel Seabury in 1784, a matter of 177 years, nobody was confirmed in America simply because there were no bishops here to confirm them. To have denied the Colonists their communion because of an obstacle they had no way of overcoming would have been an unthinkable injustice.

* "Bar Mitzvah" is the Jewish term for the ceremony at which a boy accepts adult religious responsibilities. The Bar Mitzvah is really the boy himself, but in common Jewish usage the expression has come to include the ceremony and the festive social activities that are part of the occasion.

CONSECRATION. From the Latin *sacrare*: to dedicate, plus *com:* an intensive. To set a thing or a person apart for a special religious purpose. When we use the word we are talking mainly about the consecration of

(1) bread and wine in the Holy Communion, which

then in some mystical, undefined way become the Body and Blood of Our Lord,

(2) bishops, who are thereby empowered for the office and work of the highest order of the ministry,

(3) altars, churches, Eucharistic vessels, etc., which are thus removed from secular use and from then on are treated exclusively as religious objects.

CONVENT. From the Latin *conventus:* a meeting—the same word from which we get "convention."

In ecclesiastical usage it refers to the buildings in which members of a religious community live together. Historically, it has been applied to the houses of orders of either sex, but in the popular mind it tends to mean a house of nuns.

CORPORAL. From the Latin *corpus*: body. A square piece of linen, laid on top of the altar cloth, on which the bread and wine are consecrated at the Holy Communion. Called a corporal because it holds the Body of the Lord.

COTTA. From the Middle English *coten*: to cover. A shortened form of the surplice, reaching to the waist or a little lower. Worn now mostly by choristers and acolytes.

CREDENCE. A small side table or a shelf on or in the wall on the Epistle side of the altar, to hold the bread, wine, and water to be used at the Eucharist. It is usually called the "credence table" even if it is a niche in the wall.

The word, which derives from the Latin *credo:* "I believe," seems to come from the name that was applied to the "tasting table" back in the times when

52

kings or other important personages were always in danger of being poisoned. Everything the king was to eat was first brought to a side table to be tasted by slaves. If the slaves didn't die the king could have "credence" that everything was all right and go ahead with his meal.

CREED. From the Latin *credo*: I believe. A summary, in fixed language, officially authorized by the Church, of the essential articles of Christian belief.

The purpose of a creed is both to refute heresy and to set forth truths.

See APOSTLES' CREED, NICENE CREED, ATHANASIAN CREED.

CROSIER. The shepherd's crook-shaped staff of a bishop, carried for the bishop by his chaplain and brought to him to hold when he gives absolution or blessing.

It probably started out as an ordinary walking-stick. It first appears as a liturgical ornament in the seventh century.

CRUCIFER. The person, usually a boy, who carries a cross or a crucifix at the head of an ecclesiastical procession.

It is only within the last century or so that we have had processions in our churches, which means that the crucifer is a recent development with no historical precedents to follow. Both his dress and his posture have therefore been subject over the last hundred years to the whims, tastes, and sentimentality of parish clergy, choirmothers, and choirmasters.

One would expect that under such conditions only local standards would develop, but somehow the word gets around and the silliest customs seem to have found wide acceptance.

In many parishes the crucifer is dressed in three of the Eucharistic vestments: the amice, the alb, and the girdle. All he needs to complete the full priestly garb are a stole and a chasuble, and nobody really knows why they don't put those on him, too.

To carry the cross the lad is taught to assume a position that makes it almost impossible to carry anything. He holds his elbows at 45° angles to his body. This is supposed to make the figure of the boy himself into a cross, thus adding an extra and gratuitous bit of symbolism.

And to grasp the staff of the cross he can't take hold of it naturally—he has to turn his hands around backwards. The esoteric reason for this contortion has never been divulged.

This sort of business has gone on so long now that it would take a very brave rector to instruct his crucifer to carry the cross the way he would carry any other heavy object on the end of a pole.

CRUCIFIX. A cross bearing the image of the crucified Lord.

Crucifixes dropped out of use in the Anglican church after the Reformation and were not re-introduced until the liturgical revival of the nineteenth century. See OXFORD MOVEMENT.

Among Protestants the only body that habitually uses the crucifix is the Lutheran Church.

CRUCIFORM CHURCH. From the Latin *crux*: cross, plus "form." A church built in the shape of a cross.

If you will imagine the church in a standing position, the narthex and nave are the long, upright part from the base to the lateral arms; the transepts are the arms;

and the chancel and sanctuary make up the part above the arms.

CRUET. From the old French *crue*: a vial or glass bottle. In church cruets are the vessels of glass or precious metal in which the wine and water for the Eucharist are brought to the altar.

CRYPT. From the Greek *kryptos*: hidden. A vault or cellar beneath the main floor of a church. It may be used for services of worship or for burials, or both.

In its beginnings the Church was underground in both senses of that term: it was subterrannean and it was secret. A crypt today, with its two present uses, is reminiscent of that time when Christians assembled in the catacombs to avoid detection by the civil authorities, and the tombs of the martyrs often served as altars.

CURATE. From the Latin *curatus*: the person in charge. This is also the Latin word from which museums get the title curator for their head men.

In general ecclesiastical usage it should, if literally interpreted, mean the priest in charge of a parish. But it doesn't. Somewhere along the way it lost some of its power and now when we speak of a curate we are not referring to the top man but to an assistant.

CURE. From the Latin *cura*: healing, care. A word of many meanings, most of which have to do with the field of medicine.

In church language it can mean the clergyman's function, usually expressed as "the cure of souls," or it can mean his congregation, the people committed to his care.

DEACON. From the Greek *diakonos*: servant. The lowest in rank of the three orders of the Church's ministry. See Prayer Book, page 294.

The beginning of this order is described in Acts 6: 1-6. The Apostles suddenly realized that the Christian community was getting so big that they could no longer handle both the preaching and the details of housekeeping. Specifically their complaint was, "It is not reason that we should leave the word of God and serve tables," but there was more to it than that. The poor, the widows, and the sick had to be looked after, too.

So the Apostles proposed that seven men "of honest report, full of the Holy Ghost, and wisdom" be chosen to attend to these matters and free the Apostles to devote their time "to prayer and the ministry of the word." The seven were selected and were ordained by the laying on of hands. Nowhere does the account say they were called deacons.

The Prayer Book, page 294, says "the office of a Deacon is to assist the Priest in Divine Service and in his other ministrations, under the direction of the Bishop."

DEACONESS. A disappearing kind of worker in the Church, perhaps one of the casualities of Women's Lib. The present canons do not even mention deaconesses except in their index, where they say, "see Women in Diaconate."

A deaconess used to be a "devoted unmarried woman" (to quote the old canon) appointed by the bishop to do just about anything that happened to be needed in a parish or an institution. She could be a spinster or a widow—if she married, that automatically terminated her appointment.

She wore a distinctive, identifying garb and went wherever she could make herself useful. She visited the sick and the poor, she gave Baptism and Confirmation instructions, she read Morning Prayer, Evening Prayer, and the Litany at public services, she specialized in work with women and children, and when licensed by the bishop to do so, she gave "addresses"—which means she preached. And if circumstances called for it she mopped the floor and mowed the lawn.

There are still, bless them, a few deaconesses around but their tribe will not increase. There is no longer any canonical provision for creating new ones.

DEAN. From the Latin *decanus*: ten. Originally a title given to a minor official in some supervisory capacity over a group of ten persons, for example, a monk in charge of ten novices.

Later the term gained prestige and is now applied as a title to dignitaries of considerably higher rank. In the Church there are three kinds of dean:

(1) The chief clergyman, under the bishop, of a cathedral.

(2) The head of a seminary faculty.

(3) A clergyman in a geographical division of a diocese elected or appointed to preside over various local meetings and to represent the bishop on certain ceremonial occasions, such as a groundbreaking, for example, if the bishop asks him to do so. The area in which this kind of dean holds office may, in America, be called a convocation or an archdeaconry as well as a deanery.

Today the literal "head of ten" meaning of the word is lost. If a dean turns out to be in charge of ten persons it is only accidental.

In direct address a dean in any of the three categories is called "Dean" or, sometimes in a parliamentary situation, "Mr. Dean." If you write him a letter you put "The Very Rev." before his name on the envelope and begin your letter with "Dear Dean" or "Very Reverend Sir."

DEPUTY. A delegate from a diocese to the General Convention (q.v.).

DESCENT INTO HELL, THE. The belief, based on such biblical passages as I Peter 3: 19, that Jesus, after his death, visited a place or a condition where the souls of those who had lived in pre-Christian times were waiting for the message of the Gospel.

Most theologians agree that this place or condition was not actually Hell in the ultimate sense. The Prayer Book, in the rubric preceding the Apostles' Creed (page 15 and again on page 29) gives permission to substitute "He went unto the place of departed spirits" for "He descended into hell," and says they both mean the same thing. Article 3 of the Articles of Religion (Prayer Book, page 603) is not so gentle about it. It states flatly that "he went down into Hell."

This visit is said to have occurred in the time between Christ's death and his resurrection, which confuses the issue somewhat. Jesus on the cross had told the penitent thief, "Today shalt thou be with me in Paradise" (Luke 23: 43), which seems to indicate that, wherever he and the thief went to keep their appointment, it was not the kind of place we think of as Hell. So, he descended into Hell, he went to the place of departed spirits, he went to Paradise. Our information is not very precise.

DIOCESE. From the Greek *dioikesis*: an adminis-trative division of a country. In the Church a diocese is a geographical unit. It is always under the supervi-sion of a bishop.

At first, when Christianity was chiefly an urban re-ligion, dioceses covered only the principal towns and cities. As the new faith spread, new dioceses were created and the limits of those already existing were extended. Today there is hardly any place in the world, no matter how remote, that is not within the boundaries of some diocese.

DOCTRINE. From the Latin *doctrina*: teaching. A doctrine is a teaching, a belief that is put forth as true. It is not limited to matters of religious faith—you can have a doctrine in almost any field. Freud had doc-trines, Einstein had doctrines. So did Presidents Mon-roe and Truman.

See DOGMA.

DOGMA. This is a Latin word that was derived from the Greek *dokein*: to seem good.

Its meaning is about the same as that of doctrine, that is, a belief that seems good and is therefore taught. By connotation, however, the word "dogma" carries with it the idea of authoritative support. It is not strictly true to say that a doctrine becomes a dogma when it is adopted as the official position of the Church, but that is about the way popular use of the two words works out.

Popular usage also is inclined to treat "dogma" as limited to religious belief, though literal definition does not confirm such limitation.

DOSSAL (or DORSAL). From the Latin *dorsum*: back. A piece of cloth, sometimes embroidered, hung behind the altar as a reredos (q.v.). In some parishes the dossal is in the color of the day or the season and is changed to suit the occasion.

DOXOLOGY. From the Greek *doxa*: glory. An ascription of glory to the Persons of the Holy Trinity.

The Gloria in Excelsis, Prayer Book, page 84, is known as the Greater Doxology, and the Gloria Patri (Glory be to the Father, etc.), which appears in many places and in various services in the Prayer Book, is called the Lesser Doxology. One seldom hears either of these two terms used. People usually say "the Gloria in Excelsis" or "the Gloria" when referring to one of these two doxologies.

Doxologies have also been written in metrical form as hymns, the most familiar of which is our Hymn 139: "Praise God from whom all blessings flow."

EAST. Inside the church building, east is wherever the altar is. It makes no difference what the compass says. This commonly accepted fiction, of course, makes the other end of the church west.

It is symbolic. Man instinctively thinks of the east as the realm of light, probably because that is where the sun rises. And because the sun sets in the west, the west is the region of darkness. It follows logically, then, that the altar, where Christ the Light of the World comes to us, must be in the east, and the entrance to the church, through which we come out of the dark sinful world, is in the west.

Ideally, the church should be so built that the altar really is at the east end. If this is not feasible, then it is admissible to call it east anyhow.

The baptismal font is placed near the entrance, at the west end of the nave, because it is through Holy Baptism that one comes out of darkness into light.

It was customary in earlier times for a person who was being baptized to face the west while renouncing the devil and all his works. The west was where the devil was, and one faced him while repudiating him. Then the candidate turned his back on the devil, faced the east, and declared his belief in all the Articles of the Christian Faith, as contained in the Apostles' Creed. (See Prayer Book, page 276.)

This same orientation is responsible for the current term "westward position," which means that the priest celebrating the Holy Communion stands behind the altar and faces the congregation, who are liturgically west of him.

EASTER. The festival commemorating the resurrection of Our Lord Jesus Christ. It is called Easter Day in the Book of Common Prayer, but has come to be called, redundantly, Easter Sunday by many people, including some of our own clergy and laity, and by otherwise reputable newspapers and magazines, all of whom ought to know better.

The word "Easter" is used only by English- and German-speaking peoples. It is derived from the name of the Teutonic goddess of spring: Oestra. Other languages call the day by some form of the Jewish word *Pesach* (Passover).

Easter is a movable feast (q.v.), which means that, unlike Christmas or Epiphany or any of the saints' days, for example, it does not always fall on the same calendar date. It took a long time for the Church to decide just when Easter should be observed. It was not until 325 that it was established, by the Council of Nicea, that it should always be on the Sunday on or after the full moon following the vernal equinox. By this calculation it may occur on any date from March 22 to April 25.

Easter is known as "the Queen of Festivals" not only because of its supreme status in relation to Christian theology but also because of the dependence of so much of the rest of the Christian year upon its date. The length of the Epiphany and Trinity seasons and the dates of Ash Wednesday, Holy Week, Ascension Day, Whitsunday, and Trinity Sunday are all determined by the date of Easter.

It should be noted that Easter is not only a day but also a season. As a season it is the forty days from Easter Day to Ascension Day.

ELEMENTS. The bread and wine of the Holy Communion.

EMBER DAYS. Probably a corruption, through the German *quatember*, of the Latin *quator tempora*: four seasons.

The Ember Days are four groups of three days each, the Wednesday, Friday, and Saturday following, respectively, the first Sunday in Lent, Whitsunday, September 14, and December 13. All Ember Days are fast days.

Their origin is definitely Roman. Reference to them is found as early as 220. Originally the December days were not included. The other three sets seem to have been an effort to take over and Christianize certain pagan observances connected with seed-time, harvest, and the autumn vintage.

The relation to crops has entirely faded out, and the fasting rule is obeyed by only the most austere churchmen. The days are associated now with ordinations. Also, seminarians are required to write to their bishops at each of the Ember seasons. Aside from the ordinations and the letter-writing, the Ember Days get very little attention in our time, and what they do get is only from the clergy and the clergy-to-be. The average layman might go through life without ever hearing of them.

EPIPHANY. From the Greek *epiphaneia:* a manifestation or showing, more particularly of a divine, or at least supernatural, being. The Feast of the Epiphany, celebrated on January 6, commemorates the Manifestation of Christ to the Gentiles. See Prayer Book, page 107.

The Gentiles, which is to say *we* Gentiles, are personified in this feast by the Magi, or Wise Men from the East, who were the first non-Jews to have contact with Jesus and indeed the first men of any race or nationality to be aware of his divine nature. The Epiphany therefore is a statement of the expansion of men's idea of who and what Jesus was. Throughout the Old Testament there runs the expectation of a Messiah who would someday come to be the leader of the Jews. This feast signifies the removal of any nationalistic limitation on the mission of Jesus and the recognition of him as Saviour of the whole world.

The Feast of the Epiphany began in the East as early as the third century as a memorial of the Lord's baptism in the river Jordan by St. John the Baptist. Matthew 3: 16-17 tells that on this occasion the heavens opened and a voice was heard saying, "This is my beloved Son, in whom I am well pleased." Certainly this was a "manifestation."

Within the next hundred years the commemoration had grown to include such other manifestations of Jesus's divinity as his miraculous birth, the visit of the Magi to the manger, and the water-into-wine miracle (his first) at Cana of Galilee.

When the feast was introduced into the Western part of the Church, sometime in the fourth century, the birth, baptism, and first miracle elements were dropped, leaving only the visit of the Magi, the representatives of the Gentile world.

In former times Epiphany was also called Twelfth Day, January 6 being the twelfth day after Christmas. Twelfth Night, an evening of considerable merrymaking, was the night before Twelfth Day and would therefore more properly have been called Epiphany Eve.

EPISCOPAL. From the Greek *episcopos*: overseer, bishop. "Episcopal" is the adjective in English. Anything pertaining to a bishop is episcopal. A church that has bishops is an episcopal church—for example, the Roman Catholic, the Eastern Orthodox, the Anglican, and some others. The special vestments a bishop wears are episcopal vestments, his ring is an episcopal ring, and so on.

EPISCOPATE. From the Latin *episcopus:* bishop, plus *ate:* function, or rank. The collective term for the office of bishop, as "priesthood" is the collective term for the office of priest, and "diaconate" for the office of deacon.

EPISTLES, THE. From the Greek *epistole*: a letter. Any letter is an epistle, but the word is nowadays used mostly in reference to the twenty-one letters that make up nearly half of the New Testament.

The earliest of these communications, most of which are addressed to newly-formed congregations, are the oldest of all Christian writings. They go all the way back to the days when Christianity was just getting organized. J.B. Phillips calls them "Letters to Young Churches," and that is what they were, except

64

for four of them (two to Timothy, one to Titus, and one to Philemon) that were directed to individuals.

As the early Christian missionaries founded new congregations and then moved on, leaving matters in the hands of local leaders, there often arose problems or questions or situations too complex or too hot for the local authorities to handle. So the founding fathers always tried to maintain some kind of contact with their spiritual children. When St. Paul talks about "that which cometh upon me daily: the care of all the churches" (II Corinthians 11: 28), this is what he means. He had to try to be everywhere at once.

Next to a personal visit, the best way to keep in touch was to write a letter, which is what Paul and his colleagues did. By and large, such letters were written for one of four main purposes:

(1) To deal with some local situation, like the moral laxity that was menacing the church at Corinth.

(2) To teach doctrine or argue doctrinal points. Romans and Galatians are examples here. Romans tells the Gentiles that the end of history is at hand; that Jesus, the Jewish Messiah, is the Savior of the world, and the final act of the human drama is now being played. Galatians deals with the distinction between life under the Jewish Law and life in the Spirit.

(3) To instruct or admonish, as in St. James's Epistle, the subject of which is the practice of the Christian life.

(4) To encourage the fledgling Christians, some of whom were about to meet with, or were already under, persecution. The First Epistle General of Peter is addressed to Christians in Asia Minor who were facing not only scorn from their neighbors but also a strong probability of persecution from the government.

Most of the Epistles were meant for public reading

and in some cases they were intended to be passed around from one congregation to another, which is to say they were a good deal like the Pastoral Letters bishops write today.

Besides the uses they served when they were written, the Epistles give us modern Christians many valuable bits of historical information about life in the primitive Church. From them we learn about "speaking in tongues," about the shift from the Jewish Sabbath to Sunday as the weekly holy day, about men uncovering their heads and women covering theirs during services of worship, about the practice of holding services in the people's homes, and many other things not documented elsewhere in Christian literature.

The Epistles attributed to St. Paul are, traditionally, Romans, I and II Corinthians, Galatians, Ephesians, Philippians, Colossians, I and II Thessalonians, I and II Timothy, Titus, Philemon, and Hebrews, but scholars know Paul did not write some of them and are in considerable doubt about some of the others.

The rest of the Epistles are James, I and II Peter, I, II, and III John, and Jude. About these, too, there is plenty of controversy over authorship.

ESCHATOLOGY. From the Greek *eschatos*: last. The study of "last things"—how it will all end up. The people you see on city streets carrying signs that say the world is about to end are dealing with eschatology in perhaps its simplest form.

In detail eschatology is concerned with the final destiny of both the individual and the whole human race. The manner of the world's ultimate physical destruction is not necessarily part of the subject. The field is souls, not the physical universe.

EUCHARIST. From the Greek *eucharistia*:

thanksgiving. One of the names of the sacrament known more familiarly to Episcopalians as the Holy Communion. The Church's official acceptance of the word is shown by its use in the Prayer Book, on page 574, in the first of the two rubrics at the end of the Office of Institution of Ministers.

It is not known with any historical exactness why this sacrament came to be called "thanksgiving." One explanation has been that it was so named because at its first celebration the Lord "gave thanks" over the bread and wine (Matthew 26: 26–27; I Corinthians 11: 24–25), but that seems a little strained.

A more likely reason is that as Gentile influences came into Christianity there arose a desire to find a name that would go beyond the Jewish emphasis on the sacrificial aspect of the service and give some indication of the worshippers' gratitude for all the benefits of Christ's life and death. The traditional Jewish idea about offerings to God was that they were made to placate an offended deity and persuade him to forgive.

Later Christians, not indoctrinated in the old Jewish sacrificial system, felt impelled to make their offerings as expressions of appreciation for the forgiveness that had already been freely granted them without price or persuasion.

So they saw the service as an act of thanksgiving and they called it that: the Eucharist.

See also HOLY COMMUNION, THE; LORD'S SUPPER, THE; MASS.

EVANGELISM. The proclamation of good news —any kind of good news. The root word here is the Greek *euangelos:* a bringer of good news. Christian evangelism is proclaiming the Christian message, spreading the word.

St. Paul, in Ephesians 4: 11, makes it clear that the

ability to be an evangelist is a special gift not given to all Christians. He says God has given his people various gifts "for the work of the ministry," and he lists them: "some apostles, and some prophets; some evangelists; and some pastors and teachers." The frequently expressed notion that all Christians are evangelists is not in line with St. Paul's thinking. Some of us are; others have other gifts and therefore other kinds of contributions to make to the total ministry of the Church.

The word "evangelism" does not in itself suggest any particular method of proclaiming a message. In America, however, Christian evangelism was for many years identified with a bizarre emotional technique practiced mainly by itinerant preachers skilled in working audiences into an ecstatic state that was widely accepted as evidence of a religious conversion.

Episcopalians in general found such tactics distasteful, and the Church for a while came dangerously close to rejecting evangelism itself along with its rejection of this one unacceptable form of it.

Within the last four or five decades the word has become respectable among us again, but a new distortion has replaced the old one. What is now called evangelism in the Episcopal Church would more accurately be described as a membership campaign.

The reason for the confusion is readily apparent. Isn't the purpose of evangelism to bring people into the Church? Well, then, if a congregation organizes and trains itself to make calls and bring people to Confirmation, that must be evangelism.

The basic fallacy here is the premise that church membership equals salvation, a naive and undemonstrable assumption cherished by many sincere Episcopalians. Church membership may mean nothing more than participation in a frenetic parochial busyness in which not one single religious issue is ever raised.

Going after new members—no matter how successfully—may have no relationship at all to proclaiming the Good News.

Beyond any doubt the most effective form of evangelism over the years has been the personal testimony of those who have themselves experienced conversion. Whether the conversion was instantaneous or gradual is beside the point, and not important anyway. What is important is that the man is telling his own story. He has himself met the Risen Lord and received the Holy Spirit and he is a new man living a new life. He is not arguing theology or defending the faith or quoting the Bible; he is simply saying, "This happened to me."

Remember, however, that according to St. Paul not everyone to whom the conversion experience comes has the gift of being articulate about it or the sensitivity to put it in terms that get through to the listener. Those who do have the gift are the evangelists. Their hearts can communicate with other men's hearts, opening the way for the follow-up work of the teachers and other specialists.

EWER. From, though the evolution is hard for the American ear to comprehend, the Latin *aqua*: water. The ewer's use in the church is mainly to hold the water for baptisms.

EXECUTIVE COUNCIL. You would not be far off the mark if you called this body the vestry of the national Episcopal Church.

Its forty-five members, all elected, meet three times a year on a regular schedule and can be called together at other times by the request of the Presiding

Bishop or the written request of nine Council members. Most meetings are held at Seabury House, just outside Greenwich, Connecticut.

The task of the Executive Council is a double one: (1) to carry out the program set up by the previous General Convention, and (2) to plan a three-year program to be submitted to the next General Convention. To accomplish this assignment they engage a staff of experts and specialists with offices at 815 Second Avenue, New York, New York 10017. Many people confuse the Council itself with its employees, which can and sometimes does cause either credit or blame to fall in the wrong place. It is the Council, not the staff, that takes official action.

The membership of the Council is made up as follows:

Ex officio—the Presiding Bishop and the President of the House of Deputies.

Elected by the Council itself—Vice-Presidents (normally two), the Treasurer, the Secretary.

Elected by the General Convention—six bishops, six priests, eighteen lay people.

Elected by the Provincial Synods—nine people, with no regulations about how many of them should be bishops, priests, or lay people.

The Council may fill its own vacancies, but the term of a person elected to fill a vacancy may run only until the next General Convention.

Dioceses, too, have their executive councils, organized in various ways and called by different names. To find out about yours, see your own diocesan constitution and canons.

EXORCISM. Basically this means the practice of driving out evil spirits. Pagans did it and so did the Jews, by the use of prayers and various formulas.

The custom was continued by Christians, from New

Testament times on. It was not always confined to use in connection with persons thought to be possessed by devils. Sometimes it was simply an invocation against the powers of evil. The first English Book of Common Prayer (1549) had such a prayer of exorcism in the service of Holy Baptism.

Today the Roman Church has an elaborate rite for conquering demoniac possession, a service that requires the offices of a priest, who must have the bishop's permission to do it.

The Roman service, or one much like it, is used by some of our Episcopal clergy.

FAIR LINEN. A white linen cloth cover for the altar at the Eucharist, required by the first rubric on page 67 of the Prayer Book. The rubric calls it "a fair white linen cloth." In the shorthand jargon of the clergy and altar guild members it is usually referred to simply as "the fair linen."

FASTING. To fast means to go without anything to eat or drink. It was once an important factor in Christian life, but it has now for the most part gone out of style along with most other forms of self-discipline. Ours is not an age that sees any point in making one-self uncomfortable.

The rationale of fasting is that if a man can control his appetite he can go a long way toward controlling his will. Just as the athlete uses the gymnasium to develop the body, so the religious man denies himself the pleasures of the table in order to strengthen his spiritual muscles.

Fasting has been a standard part of man's religious life as far back as the records go. At first he did it for mistaken or naive reasons. Prolonged periods of hunger often produce hallucinations, which primitive man took to be direct contacts with the spirit world. So he frequently gave up eating in order to put himself in touch with the supernatural.

He had other reasons, too. A man voluntarily suffering from hunger might be showing how pious he was, or he might be trying to arouse the sympathy or the forbearance of the gods. Or he might be demonstrating penitence.

The great religions are psychologically more sound and sophisticated about it; they see it as spiritual exercise.

Jesus assumed that people fasted. In his Sermon on the Mount he said "When ye fast," not "If ye fast" (St. Matthew 6: 16).

The Church, too, assumes that we fast. On page li in the front of the Prayer Book there is a Table of Fasts, in which Ash Wednesday and Good Friday stand alone, indicating that they are "absolute" fasts. Traditionally, this means that, health permitting, we are to take neither food nor drink until "the ninth hour," that is, 3:00 P.M.

The Table then goes on to list other days "on which the Church requires such a measure of abstinence as is more especially suited to extraordinary acts and exercises of devotion."

Thus a distinction is made between fasting and abstinence. Abstinence may or may not involve food. It is more likely to be concerned with giving up luxuries, pleasures, amusements, entertainments, and social events.

The main point to be remembered about both fast-

72

ing and abstinence is that their purpose is not to deprive us of our joys but to help our higher nature gain dominance over the lower. As in most cases, when people think the Church is imposing a harsh rule on them she is really giving them some friendly advice.

FONT. From the Latin *fons*: a spring of water. The receptacle for baptismal water, usually made of stone.

In early times, when adult baptism by immersion* was the rule, the font was a large basin below ground level, big enough for the candidate to stand in while the water was poured over him.

When infant baptism became the norm and affusion* the prevalent form, fonts became higher and smaller and took on their present cup shape.

Because one comes into the Christian Church through the Sacrament of Holy Baptism, the proper place for the font is at the "west" end of the church building, near the entrance.

* See under BAPTISM.

FRIAR. From the Latin *frater*: brother. A member of a men's religious order.

FRONTAL. The panel of embroidered cloth, most often silk, that hangs down the front of an altar. It is usually changeable and its color agrees with the liturgical color of the season or the day.

A frontal covers the entire front of the altar, from side to side and top to floor. Not all parishes have full frontals for their altars—small parishes just can't afford them. So they make do with what is called a superfrontal, an abbreviated form that hangs down only a few inches.

More affluent parishes may have both a frontal and a superfrontal on the altar.

GENERAL CONVENTION. The top legislative and program-planning body of the Episcopal Church. It is required by canon to meet every three years and may be called into special meetings between regular sessions.

The General Convention is in structure something like the British Parliament. It sits in two Houses: the House of Bishops, which resembles the House of Lords in that its members do not run for re-election, and the House of Deputies, whose members are chosen (their dioceses decide how) for single terms of three years each. This latter House is comparable to the House of Commons.

The House of Deputies is composed of four clergymen and four lay persons from each diocese, which gives it a membership of almost one thousand. It elects its own President, who does what he can about keeping a thousand people in order and concerned with the agenda. One delaying tactic that often frustrates him is the House's privilege of having a vote on certain kinds of questions taken "by orders." After a close vote on such issues anyone on the losing side can ask that a recount be taken, this time with clergy and laity voting separately. In such cases a majority of both orders is needed to put the question over. It is a long, tedious process and most of the time it doesn't change the original vote.

Except for the election of a Presiding Bishop, an action may originate in either House, and if it passes it is sent on to the other House for concurrence. The Deputies cannot elect a Presiding Bishop, but they can veto the one the Bishops elect. No action of any kind can be passed without the approval of both Houses.

The General Convention, with its unwieldy numbers and its short working time (about two weeks) cannot possibly handle all the legislation, program proposals, Prayer Book revisions, etc., that are brought before it. For this reason it sets up many Joint Committees and Commissions ("joint" means that members are drawn from both Houses) to go on working through the next three years and report back to the next General Convention.

GENUFLECTION. From the Latin *genu*: knee, plus *flectere*: to bend. A genuflection is a sort of deep curtsey—so deep that the right knee touches the floor.

Probably fewer than half of our people genuflect, but if you do it, following are the proper times:

(1) When passing before the Reserved Sacrament,
(2) When entering or leaving your pew when the consecrated bread and wine are on the altar,
(3) When the words "who for us men and for our salvation," etc., are said in the Nicene Creed. (This passage in the Creed is called the *Incarnatus*.)

GLORIA IN EXCELSIS. The first words, in Latin, of the familiar hymn on page 84 of the Prayer Book. Its translation is "Glory be to God on high." It is Greek in origin, but nobody knows when it was written or who wrote it.

The Gloria in Excelsis is in the wrong place in our Eucharist. Traditionally it should come right after the Kyrie ("Lord have mercy") on page 70. That's where it is in the Roman Mass and that's where it was in Cranmer's Prayer Book of 1549. Why it was moved to its present position and why it is "high church" to want it back where it belongs is not clear.

GLORIA PATRI. Latin for the first words of "Glory be to the Father, and to the Son, and to the Holy Ghost." We use it mostly at the end of a Psalm or series of Psalms. It was put there perhaps as early as the fourth century, to "Christianize" these purely Jewish hymns.

The Puritans, when they took over the Church of England (1653–1660), refused to use the Gloria because it is not scriptural, that is, it does not appear verbatim anywhere in the Bible. It was put back into the Prayer Book when the monarchy was restored in 1660.

GLOSSALALIA. From two Greek words— *glossa:* tongue, and *lalein:* to talk. Popularly known as "speaking in tongues."

The utterance of untranslatable syllables and sounds by one in a trance-like state of religious ecstasy.

This phenomenon is often misunderstood as an ability to speak foreign languages without ever having had to learn them. This error comes from St. Luke's overenthusiastic account of what happened on Pentecost—see Acts 2. Later New Testament references to speaking in tongues show that it amounted to a series of meaningless sounds, an inspired gibberish, not words from any language.

St. Paul goes into it in considerable detail in the twelfth and fourteenth chapters of his First Epistle to the Corinthians. Paul himself seems to have had an exceptional gift for such speaking. He believed it was a heavenly language. The speaker, he thought, is speaking to God; his speech needs no translation.

Paul makes a distinction between speaking in tongues in church and speaking so when one is alone. He says one man has the gift of speaking and another the gift of interpreting, and if you don't have an interpreter around and can't interpret for yourself, then don't speak in church. What you say is of no use to others. Save it for times when there are no others present to be confused and frustrated by it.

There was a time in the early Church when glossalalia was expected, indeed almost required, as evidence of having received the Holy Ghost. In recent years there has been a revival of interest in it in the Episcopal Church, and in some places it has become a highly controversial subject. There seems to be no neutral ground. Those who don't believe in it say it is crazy; those who do say it is the ultimate union with the Holy Ghost.

Psychiatry regards it as a hypnotic manifestation resulting from religious excitement.

GODPARENT. A godparent, that is, a godfather or godmother, is a person who sponsors a child at baptism. Ordinarily a boy has two godfathers and one godmother, a girl two godmothers and one godfather. But in our American church it is not absolutely required that there be any. The Prayer Book says, "when they can be had."

There have been sponsors in baptism at least since the beginning of the third century, perhaps before that. In those ancient times, however, the sponsor's function was quite different from what it is today. Most of the candidates for baptism were adults, and to sponsor one of them meant chiefly to testify to his character and sincerity and to assure the congregation that he was not a police spy infiltrating the group just to gather names for the authorities.

Nowadays godparents are needed only when the candidate is too young to speak for himself. They alternate between representing the child and representing the congregation that is receiving him. They speak for the child in answering the questions on page 276 and at the top of page 277; they speak for the congregation (of which they are a part) when they answer the two questions at the middle of page 277.

It is these latter two questions that delineate the sponsors' continuing duties. The whole congregation receives the child, but the sponsors, as their agents, take personal responsibility for his Christian education and his eventual presentation to the bishop to be confirmed.

Why sponsors are called godparents is not explained anywhere, probably because the explanation is so obvious. Sponsors are "spiritual parents," through whose action the child is "born again," this time into the Christian family.

GOOD FRIDAY. See under HOLY WEEK.

GOSPEL, THE. From the Anglo-Saxon *godspel:* good news. The term is applied by English-speaking peoples to the message of Jesus. After 1900 years it is hard for us to think of that message as news, but at the time Jesus delivered it, it was a radically new concept of the relationship between God and man.

Up to that time the idea had been, "Be good and you will be saved." Man's salvation was a matter of God's response to man's righteousness. And that was very bad news, because, as Jesus pointed out in the Sermon on the Mount, true goodness involves not only outward behavior but also inner feeling, and though one may be able to go through the right motions one's feelings are beyond control.

The good news that Jesus introduced is that God loves us as we are—unlovable, corrupt, sinful. We cannot possibly earn his love by any merit of our own because we don't have any merit. But we don't have to. The Lord says he stands at our door and knocks, asking to be let in. Opening the door and letting him in is not as simple as it sounds, for it includes such things as repentance, surrender, submission, and giving up our illusions of self-sufficiency, but the point is that the initiative is his, not ours. Our job is not to impress him but to accept his offer and thank him.

Whether we are striving to live up to our end of a deal with him or trying to show how grateful we are that he doesn't hold us to any deal, we will still work hard to be good. But being good to placate him and being good to please him are by no means the same thing. There is a vast difference between keeping rules and responding to love, because there is a 180° difference in the motivation.

To a world bogged down in hopeless striving, that was, and still is, good news.

GOSPELS, THE. The first four books of the New Testament. In English translations these books are known, respectively, as the Gospel according to Matthew, Mark, Luke, and John.

The title may come from the fact that the book of Mark, the earliest of the four, in its opening sentence calls itself "the gospel of Jesus Christ," and a few verses later (1: 14) identifies the theme of Christ's preaching as "the gospel of the kingdom of God." It then goes on with reports of his preaching, together with biographical details and accounts of events that took place during his ministry, thus setting the general pattern for the later books of Matthew and Luke. John's Gospel differs from the other three in that it includes meditations and interpretations. It does not pretend to be "straight reporting."

Matthew, Mark, and Luke are called the Synoptic ("with the same eye") Gospels because their narratives are all built on the same events in the life of Jesus. John stands somewhat apart because of the author's more subjective approach. The four books together are called the Four Gospels.

It should be noted that none of the Gospels can be taken as a biography in the modern sense. They are not written from the objective point of view of today's biographical scholar. Their purpose was a partisan one: to strengthen the faith of the early Christians by providing them with a written body of traditional lore about their Master. The material they present does furnish a realistic historical picture of Jesus, but it by no means amounts to an impartial or complete record of his life.

Mark, the briefest of the four, was, as noted above, the first one written. Most scholars date it anywhere from 65 to 75, and say the author's purpose was to encourage the Christians during the crisis caused by Nero's persecutions.

According to tradition Mark got his material by talking with St. Peter and taking notes on the Apostle's reminiscences, which would certainly give the book first-rate credentials. But there are respected authorities who find a Gentile point of view in Mark's writing. They believe the author was a Gentile and that his purpose was to get the Christian message out of the rigidly Jewish terms in which it was first presented. They assert that what he got from Peter he got from Peter's sermons, not from conversations, and they point out that he was not in much awe of Peter or any of the other Apostles. He thought they didn't understand Jesus very well.

His name, they say, may have been Mark, but they doubt that he was the John Mark to whom the book's authorship has commonly been ascribed.

Matthew's Gospel, scholars agree, was not written by the Apostle Matthew. It is dated between 80 and 100, and since it draws on Mark for its biographical sections, that substantiates the 65-75 date for Mark.

Matthew had access also to a collection of sayings of

Jesus, which has now long been lost. Scholars call the collection "Q," which doesn't explain anything. It is only the abbreviation for the German word *Quelle*, which means "source."

The author's special purpose in this Gospel was to show that Jesus was indeed the long-expected Jewish Messiah, that in him the Old Testament prophecies had been fulfilled. This is why in Matthew one so frequently finds some form of the statement: "all this was done that it might be fulfilled which was spoken by the prophet . . . ."

Only in Matthew's Gospel are we told about the Wise Men coming from the East and about Jesus calling Peter the rock on which the Church would be built. It is also from Matthew that we get most of what is recorded of Christ's Sermon on the Mount.

Luke's Gospel is the longest and most delicately literary of the four. It is written in excellent Greek, obviously done by a sensitive, educated man. The best estimate as to its date is 85 to 95.

The book is the first of a two-volume work (Acts is the other part), both addressed to some evidently high-ranking personage named Theophilus, but certainly intended for a wider readership. According to an early tradition, the author was St. Luke, the Gentile physician who was the travel companion of St. Paul.

Luke's purpose, stated in his introduction (1: 1–4) was to organize and supplement for Theophilus the writings of others who had already undertaken "to set forth in order a declaration of those things which are most surely believed among us."

As sources he had Mark and Q, but about a quarter of his material comes from some other collection or collections. Only Luke, for example, gives us such treasures as the parables of the Prodigal Son and the Good Samaritan, the story of the Penitent Thief who was crucified with Jesus, and the lovely poetry of the Magnificat and the Nunc Dimittis. And it is Luke who, more than any other Gospel writer, shows us the loving care Jesus had for the poor and the outcast and presents him as bringing salvation to those who needed it most: publicans, sinners, Samaritans, and Gentiles.

The Gospel of John is the latest of the four, having possibly been written in the early years of the second century. There is a strong tradition that the Apostle John was the author, but its late date of composition makes this questionable.

One solution to the problem of how John could have been the author of a book that was written when he was senile, if not already dead, is that he had at an earlier time written, or some say dictated, a first draft of his Gospel and that it was elaborated and published after his death. This theory would also help to clear up another puzzle: the Gospel is full of Jewish idiom, yet its language is fine, grammatical Greek. John's Gospel was transcribed or edited or put into its final form by a Greek collaborator—is that how it was?

As to his sources, scholars do not agree on whether he owed anything to Mark and Luke. Some find evidence that he did; others see no such signs. Tradition holds that the whole book is one hundred per cent the product of John's own memory.

His purpose in writing was evangelistic. He says so himself in chapter 20, verse 31. These things are written "that ye may believe that Jesus is the Christ, the Son of God, and that believing ye might have life through his name."

GRACE. From the Latin *gratus:* favorable, pleasing. A very simple word, only vaguely understood in its theological sense. It refers to God's love for sinful man.

Man cannot earn God's love. We cannot be good

enough to deserve salvation. But because he loves us he helps us to do what we cannot do on our own. The collect for the Second Sunday in Lent says, "Who seest that we have no power of ourselves to help ourselves," and that is precisely the predicament we are in. This is where grace comes in. God, in his love for us, gives us the power to be better than our frail nature will let us be.

Grace comes to us through prayer, through reading the Scripture, and especially through receiving the Holy Communion. We have to seek it, to be sure, but millions of Christians can testify that when one does seek it God gives it abundantly.

It's that simple—and that tremendous. Grace is the undeserved help we get from God, free to anyone who seriously tries for it.

GRADUAL. In the early Church hymns or Psalms were frequently sung between the Epistle and the Gospel in the Holy Communion service. This chant took its name from the step (Latin: *gradus*) from which it was sung.

In the first English Book of Common Prayer, 1549, the Gradual was dropped, for reasons not now known. It was restored to the American liturgy in our revision of 1928. See the rubric at the middle of page 70—"Here may be sung a Hymn or an Anthem."

The Gradual is now sung either by the choir or by the congregation.

HABIT. A distinctive form of dress worn by members of religious orders. Normally it consists of a tunic, a belt or girdle, and a sleeveless cloak hanging almost to the feet, called a scapular. A hood is attached to men's habits. Women's headcoverings range from veils to elaborate heavily starched linen headdresses.

Women's orders have greatly modified and modernized their habits in recent years, and some of the men's orders have dispensed with habits for traveling or entirely.

HAGIOLOGY. From the Greek *hagios:* holy, and *logos:* word. Literally "the word about the holy ones." Less literally, "the study of the saints."

This study finds expression in two forms:
(1) A history or description of the saints or their writings,
(2) A catalog of the saints.

Either of these would be called a hagiography. The person who produced them would be a hagiographer.

HIERARCHY. From the Greek *hieros:* sacred, and *archos:* leader. Hierarchy is not an exclusively ecclesiastic word. It can be applied to any organization that is administered by an authoritarian group: a business firm, a school, the army, etc. But it is used mostly in connection with the Church, and here it means the chain of command, the organization of the clergy by rank and jurisdiction.

The hierarchy in the Episcopal Church is:
(1) The Presiding Bishop,
(2) All other bishops,
(3) Priests,
(4) Deacons.

HOLY COMMUNION, THE. The title most commonly applied to the Sacrament of the Body and Blood of Christ, also known as the Eucharist, the Lord's Supper, and the Mass.

84

Each title has its own special shade of emphasis. Here the stress is on the union between Christ and the person who receives him in the Sacrament, the union between all such persons and one another, and the union between the whole Church and its Lord.

HOLY OIL. See under CHRISM.

HOLY ORDERS. The three ranks of the Christian ministry: the episcopate, the priesthood, and the diaconate. Bishops, priests, and deacons are said to be "in Holy Orders."

Not to be confused with "Religious Orders," which is a term reserved for monastic societies.

HOLY SATURDAY. See under HOLY WEEK.

HOLY WATER. We don't do much about holy water in most Episcopal churches. In a sense the water from a baptism might be called holy. If a priest performed the baptism he blessed the water. So also might the water left in the cruet after a service of Holy Communion. It was blessed before some of it was mixed with the wine. Whether it's holy or not, the water in both these cases is considered different enough from ordinary water that it is poured out on the ground instead of down the drain.

But that is not what is meant, strictly, by the term holy water. Holy water is water that has been blessed by a priest for use in exorcisms (q.v.), dedications, burials, and ceremonial washings such as the Asperges, that is, the sprinkling of the altar and of the congregation before the principal Mass on Sunday, and the self-cleansing sign of the cross made after dipping the fingers in the holy water stoup on entering a church.

Salt that has been blessed is added to the water

used in these rites.

Such ceremonies are practiced chiefly in the Roman Church, but there are some Anglican churches in which they are performed.

HOLY WEEK. The week preceding Easter, that is, the last week in Lent. It is observed in both East and West—though usually their dates are different—in remembrance of the last week of the Lord's life as a man on earth.

Each day of Holy Week has its special character and five of the days have special names.

The days of the week are:

Palm Sunday, which commemorates Christ's "triumphal entry into Jerusalem," with shouting crowds laying palm branches in His path. The events of the ensuing days proved the triumph to be a hollow one. On that Sunday the city was filled with pilgrims who had come to town for the Passover, all in holiday mood, roaming the streets looking for entertainment and ready to join in anything that promised to be fun. John 12: 12-14 makes it appear that the people recognized and welcomed Jesus as "the King of Israel." If they did they soon forgot him.

Monday, with no distinguishing name of its own, the day when Jesus had his famous run-in with the money-changers in the Temple (Matthew 21: 12–13).

Tuesday, also without a special title, the day that gave us the "render unto Caesar" that has become part of our everyday speech (Luke 20: 22–25). Jesus spent part of this day teaching in the Temple. Toward evening he stood on a hill outside the city, weeping over it and foretelling its destruction.

Spy Wednesday, so called because it was the day on which Judas Iscariot made his deal with the priests, promising for thirty pieces of silver (about $20) to bring them to the place where they could arrest Jesus without risking a public disturbance (Matthew 26: 14).

Maundy Thursday, which is actually Commaundment Thursday. Commandment used to have a "u" in it. It got shortened to maundy through careless enunciation. The day was so named because on this evening Jesus said to his disciples, "A new commandment I give unto you, that ye love one another" (John 13:34). This was also the evening on which he washed the disciples' feet (John 13: 5). Most important of all, it was the evening of the Last Supper, the beginning of the Holy Communion, which is Christianity's central sacrament (Matthew 26: 20–30).

Good Friday, the day he was tried, crucified, and laid in the tomb. It is not clear why a day of such infamy should be called good. Some say it is because of the great benefits that accrued to man through Christ's passion and death; some believe it was originally "God's Friday" but slipped into "Good Friday" the same way "commaundment" slipped into "maundy."

Holy Saturday, or Easter Even, the one full day the body of Christ lay in the tomb, while his spirit, according to the Apostles' Creed, descended into hell.

HOST. From the Latin *hostia:* a sacrificial victim. The term used for the consecrated bread in the Holy Communion. It implies belief in the dogma of Transubstantiation, that is, belief that the bread, after being consecrated by a priest, literally *is* the sacrificed body of Christ.

In general usage, however, the word is applied to all altar bread, whether consecrated or not. The ladies of the Altar Guild talk about "priest's hosts" and "people's hosts" as simply part of their altar supplies. (The priest's host is larger than the ones administered to the congregation.)

The host is made of unleavened bread.

HYMN. From the Greek *hymnos:* song of praise. A poem or other metrical composition adapted for singing in a religious service. A carol, an anthem, a religious song.

As time goes in church history, it is only yesterday that hymns began to be sung in Anglican churches. Canticles and Psalms were sung, but devotional or topical verse set to music was considered illegal. Not that there was any law against it; there just wasn't any rubric that permitted it. The Church of England has a reputation, not entirely unearned, for being a bit stuffy at times. Anything new is per se frivolous. Hymns had never been sung in church, therefore hymns could never be sung in church.

The Wesley brothers, John and Charles, with their great outdoor evangelistic meetings, realized the value of congregational singing. Charles wrote many excellent hymns, and the brothers imported others from foreign countries. They became an important part of the Wesleyan method of involving the people in the revival that swept over England in the latter half of the eighteenth century. Congregations sang heartily—everywhere except in the Church of England.

By the end of the eighteenth century some of the more daring English clergy were defying the authorities and introducing hymns into their regular services of worship. When, in 1820, the vicar of St. Paul's, Sheffield, published a hymnbook for use in his parish, his action provided a test case. The times were in the good vicar's favor. Everybody wanted to sing hymns in church. The vicar was acquitted of any wrongdoing and hymns were approved for use in the dignified Church of England.

Hymns are so natural a part of our services now that it is hard to realize they were forbidden up to only 150 years ago.

The word "hymn" is sometimes encountered as a verb. "To hymn" means "to praise or worship by singing."

I, J, and K

INCENSE. From the Latin *incendere:* to burn. Incense is used in many religious rites, not all of them Christian. The smoke from it symbolizes prayer rising to Heaven. The Jews burned incense in the Temple, but there is no clear evidence of Christians using it until around the year 500.

INSTITUTION, OFFICE OF. The admission of a new incumbent to the spiritual leadership of a parish. The form for this ceremony begins on page 569 of the Prayer Book.

It is customary for the bishop to officiate at this service, but he may appoint a priest to act in his stead.

There is nothing mandatory about the use of the Office of Institution. Many a new rector takes charge of his parish without being formally instituted, and his powers and authority are exactly the same as if he had gone through the public ceremony.

It is, however, a popular service and is widely if not universally used. Even though it is not required, it is thought by many to have a good psychological effect because it involves the whole congregation as witnesses to the bishop's commissioning of the new rector and the vestry's acceptance of him.

INTINCTION. From the Latin *intingere:* to dip. The practice of dipping the consecrated bread into the consecrated wine by a person receiving the Holy Communion. (Sometimes the priest dips it for him and puts it on his tongue.)

Intinction evidently began in the Communion of the Sick, in tuberculosis sanitaria or in various situations where contagion was feared. Now many germ-conscious people never receive any other way. The clergy, who have to drink from the chalice after everyone else has received, don't seem especially prone to plagues and epidemics.

There is no place in the Prayer Book or the Canons where this form of administration is specifically permitted or specifically prohibited.

INTROIT. From the Latin *introitus:* entrance. A brief ceremony used at the beginning of the Mass in the Roman Church, sometimes in the Anglican.

It is said by the priest, or if there is a choir, it is sung.

It consists of a Psalm, or some verses of a Psalm, an Antiphon, (q.v.) and the Gloria Patri (q.v.).

JUDGMENT DAY. Both the Nicene and Apostles' Creeds say that Jesus will come to judge the quick and the dead. It is therefore an article of faith, a required belief, that there will come a time when everyone living and dead, will be called up to judgment.

The popular idea of what it will be like has been grotesquely distorted from earliest times right down to the present. Unfortunately, we have never gotten over the idea of salvation by merit. In spite of the Gospel, the good news that loves both saints and sinners, we cling to the notion that we must earn our way to eternal life. After two thousand years of Christianity we still have not got it through our heads that God's love is a free gift, not part of a deal. We go on thinking that God accepts the man who keeps the Law and rejects the man who does not.

In the minds of many people the Judgment Day is a sort of graduation day. Those who have assiduously done their homework will receive their diplomas, which will admit them to celestial bliss throughout never-ending time. The flunk-outs will be sent to some vague place of everlasting punishment, which we half-facetiously associate with excessive heat. This, on the face of it, is inconsistent with the Christian concept of a God who loves his whole creation.

Jesus, in the Sermon on the Mount, made clear how impossible it is for a man to keep the Law in his heart even though he may manage to adhere to the letter of it in his external action. St. Paul declared that we are not good, that the Law and our sinful nature are often in basic conflict, but that God loves us even in our sin. What chance would any of us have if only the sinless were to be saved?

Bishop Spencer, of West Missouri, speaking in the courtroom metaphor, used to say that the court on Judgment Day would be "rigged" in our favor. "The judge," he said, "will also be counsel for the defense."

There is another way of thinking about Judgment Day. Suppose it is a day when God lets you and me do the judging? Suppose it is the day when we are allowed to decide whether we could stand to live throughout all eternity in the shattering light of God's absolute perfection. Or would we be more comfortable elsewhere? Even Judas was allowed "to go to his

91

own place" (Acts 1: 25). So will God in his mercy allow us to go, if the prospect of staying is too overwhelming for us.

Who could live in the presence of that perfection forever? Certainly not those who come to the Judgment Day as self-conscious strangers, never having known him. Not those who come filled with guilt because his forgiveness has never been a reality to them. Rather it will be those who already know something about what living with him is from having lived with him in this life, who have accepted his forgiveness and devoted themselves to responding to his love. To those who have spent their lives on this earth in God's presence, spending eternity with him will be a growth and a fulfillment. To others the same situation would be hell.

The Church does not go into any detail about the form in which we will appear when we rise for the Judgment Day. St. Paul holds up a contrast between the way it is here and the way it will be later. "Now," he says, "we see through a glass, darkly, but then face to face: now I know in part; but then I shall know even as I am known" (I Corinthians 13: 12). This says nothing about what we will look like, but it is an unmistakable assertion that we will have identity and communication. And what else could we need?

KYRIE ELEISON. Greek for "Lord have mercy." A short hymn that comes at the beginning of the Eucharist. (Prayer Book, top of page 70.)

The form is threefold:

> Lord, have mercy upon us.
> Christ, have mercy upon us.
> Lord, have mercy upon us.

The Kyrie also appears in the Litany, Prayer Book, bottom of page 57.

L

LAITY, MINISTRY OF THE. To define this part of the Christian layman's responsibility it is necessary first to draw a distinction between jobs and ministry, between what a man does *for* the Church and what he does *as* the Church. "Church work" is not the same thing as "the work of the Church."

It is obvious to everyone that the layman has certain chores to do *for* the Church: such things as ushering, serving on the vestry, raising the budget, singing in the choir, and the like. These are his jobs, his "church work."

He also has a ministry above and beyond these duties. When you say "ministry" in connection with the laity, people's minds automatically turn to such matters as layreading and serving at the altar. "Minister" to most of us equals man wearing vestments and taking part in a service of public worship. So, if we perceive that a layman has a ministry beyond his jobs we assume that he is performing it when he puts on a cassock and surplice and reads the lessons or preaches or administers the chalice.

The point to be made here is that neither doing church jobs nor participating in the leadership of public services is the ministry of the laity. What, then, is this ministry?

Probably the best way to get at it is to look at St. Paul's list of the talents and specialities that are involved in the Church's total ministry. In Ephesians 4: 11 St. Paul tells what abilities Christ has given his people *"for the work of the ministry."* He says, "And he gave some apostles; and some prophets; and some evangelists; and some pastors and teachers. . . ."

The modern equivalent of "apostles" would be the ordained clergy—a very tiny segment of the Church's work force. The clergy make up about one-half of one per cent of the membership of the whole Christian Church, Catholic, Orthodox, and Protestant. That means that the rest of the ministering—the prophesying, the evangelizing, and so on—is to be done by the 99.5 per cent who are laymen. And according to St. Paul, some have the talents for one activity, some for another. Some are equipped for more than one. But whatever a man's equipment may be, it is given to him by Christ, and given for a specific purpose.

Webster says prophecy is "the declaration of the divine will and purpose." People by and large think that to prophesy is to foretell the future, but "prediction" is third on Webster's list of what the word means.* What prophecy really boils down to is the ability to discern and be articulate about God's action in the events of one's own life and in the corporate life of the community. Not many people can do that, but we all know people to whom it seems to come naturally. That is their ministry, their part of the Church's ministry.

The Holy Spirit has also enabled some to recognize the signs when someone they know is ready to hear what Christ can do in an individual's life when he takes it over. This perception, together with the ability to speak the opening word, is the gift of the

* It is not hard to understand how prophecy came to be confused with prediction in people's minds. When the Old Testament prophets said such and such a thing was going to happen they were not actually forecasting a coming event. Usually they were sounding a warning: this is where your present course will lead you, this is how it will be *unless*—unless you change your ways, unless you shape up, unless you get back into conformity with the will of God. And usually the people did not shape up, and the thing the prophet had warned them about *did* happen and the prophet got credit for being able to predict the future.

evangelist. No evangelist ever converted anyone. Men don't convert men; the Holy Spirit does the converting. The evangelist's task is to spot them at the crucial moment and bring them into the Christian community, where conversion can take place. If he can bring them into this milieu and let the other lay ministers—the pastors and the teachers—take over, he has done what an evangelist is supposed to do.

"To some pastors." Here is a category of the ministry that most of us automatically assign to the clergy. Some denominations even give the local clergyman the formal title of "Pastor." The word itself means "shepherd," and there is no question but that our Prayer Book supports the idea that a parish clergyman has a "flock" committed to his care. It is also true that some clergymen are not good pastors. The gift was not given to them.

In its deepest sense, to be a pastor is to have the gift of helping sick or troubled souls. It is the ability to listen, to understand, to take on a share of the burden and to stay with it until, with the help of God, relief and then victory are achieved. A pecular sensitivity is needed, an aptitude for putting oneself in the other person's shoes and for communicating one's own concern and sustaining strength.

Certainly not every layman or woman has this combination of endowments. But there are those who do; we all know some who do. They are the ones Christ has given the capacity to be pastors. That is their specialty in the work of the ministry.

"And teachers." Teaching is the one part of the Church's ministry that we have no difficulty in allocating to the laity. True, we are likely to think of it as Sunday School teaching or conducting a Bible class, but we do think the laity can teach.

But Christianity itself is not subject matter. Christian faith is caught, not taught. What, then, is a Christian teacher, one whose teaching is a ministry? It comes to something like this: there are, as our Prayer Book says, "things which a Christian ought to know and believe to his soul's health." A teacher is one who can not only tell him the facts about his faith—its history, its meaning, its daily application—but can tell him in such a way that the process is not just an imparting of information but a meeting of hearts, and its content is related not just to the mind's store but to the soul's health. The ability to teach this way is a gift. Doing it is ministry.

So there it is—the work of the ministry, for which Christ has given his people the various necessary gifts. There are the sacramental, the prophetic, the evangelistic, the pastoral, and the tutorial aspects of this ministry—these five, and the last four are for the most part in the hands of the laity.

LAMBETH CONFERENCE. A meeting of all Anglican bishops from around the world, held approximately every ten years. The Conference is called and chaired by the Archbishop of Canterbury. It gets the name Lambeth Conference because it meets at Lambeth Palace, the Archbishop's London residence.

The Anglican Communion has no central government. It is rather a free association of twenty-one autonomous national Churches. The Lambeth Conference is the chief instrument through which a vital relationship among these twenty-one Churches is maintained.

The conference has no authority to enforce any of its opinions or resolutions on any of the participating Churches. Its objective has been stated as bringing together "the Anglican bishops exercising jurisdiction throughout the world for the purpose of taking common council and adopting reports and resolutions of an advisory nature for the guidance of its national

Churches, Provinces, and Dioceses."* Of course this includes our American bishops. The conference has neither legislative nor executive powers, but its actions have a tremendous influence on the life of the whole Anglican Communion.

The first Lambeth Conference was held in 1867. Since then it has met at approximate ten-year intervals except for the gap from 1930 to 1948, caused by World War II.

LAMBETH QUADRILATERAL. This four-point statement was for a while known as the Chicago Quadrilateral. It was formulated by our American General Convention at Chicago in 1886 for the purpose of setting forth the essential requirements for a united Christian Church. They are as follows:

(1) belief in the Apostles' and Nicene Creeds,
(2) belief in the Holy Scriptures,
(3) continuation in the Historic Ministry,
(4) acceptance of Holy Baptism and the Holy Communion as sacraments instituted by Christ himself.

This statement was produced as a result of the movement toward Church Unity, which was in the air even then. General Convention was saying, in effect, that the Episcopal Church was ready to discuss unity, but unless the other party to the discussion acknowledged these four elements as basic and indispensable there was no use even starting any talks.

Two years later, at the 1888 Lambeth Conference, 145 bishops from all over the world approved the Chicago statement and it became the Lambeth Quadrilateral. With this Lambeth approval the Quadrilateral comes as close as any pronouncement can to

* *Episcopal Church Annual.*

representing the official position of the worldwide Anglican Communion.

LAVABO. In Latin this is "I will wash." Lavabo means the ceremonial cleansing of the celebrant's fingers at the Eucharist. The word also is applied to the bowl or basin in which this washing is done.

LAYMAN. From the Greek *laos:* people. Originally used to distinguish between clergymen and those who were not clergymen. Anyone who was not an ordained minister was a layman.

The word still has this original meaning in church parlance, but it has been adopted also by professions, trades, and all kinds of specialized groups to designate persons who are outside the group's own particular field. Medical doctors, for example, call everyone who is not a doctor a layman. The same practice is followed by lawyers and scientists, and probably by interior decorators and disc jockeys. You can't help being a layman in somebody's view.

LAYREADER. A layman licensed by the bishop to conduct religious services. That was all a layreader was permitted to do when the first one was licensed in 1866 by the Bishop of Gloucester.

Gradually the privileges of the office have been expanded. Now a layreader may read the Epistle and administer the chalice at the Eucharist, and in cases where a mission would otherwise be without leadership may be assigned to complete charge and even put in residence. Some are permitted to preach, but only rarely may a layreader's sermons be of his own composition.

He may not under any circumstances give absolution or blessing, consecrate the bread and wine, perform marriages, or baptize—except in those emergencies where any layman, licensed or not, may baptize.

LECTERN. From the Latin *legere:* to read. Literally, a lectern is a reading desk, a stand of some sort on which someone places something he wants to read.

Every hotel meeting room, every convention hall, every place where people make speeches has a lectern on which speakers rest their notes or manuscripts. The word seems, however, to be especially related to the lectern's ecclesiastical use, and some dictionaries say only that it is the reading desk in a church from which the Scriptures are read.

In the Episcopal Church the lectern may be as plain as a wooden box or as elaborate as a carved stone eagle. That makes no difference. Plain or fancy, it is still a lectern.

Note that in small churches, particularly missions, the lectern frequently serves also as a pulpit.

See PULPIT.

LECTIONARY. From the Latin *legere:* to read. Tables of lessons and Psalms appointed to be read at services throughout the year. The lectionary for Morning and Evening Prayer is found in the front part of the Prayer Book, the part where the pages are in Roman numerals—see pages *x* to *xlv*.

LENT. From the Anglo-Saxon *lencten:* spring, the time of lengthening days. Lent is the forty-day penitential season beginning on Ash Wednesday and ending on Easter Eve.

Until quite recent years Lent was observed by enough people and with enough seriousness that the pace of our common life was manifestly slowed down during these forty days. Now the small recognition it receives is scarcely more than a token.

Lent began to disappear from the American scene when self-denial began to disappear. Devotional exercises are considered pointless calisthenics because their "relevance" to social issues is not immediately discernible. The idea that a single, serious, self-disciplined Christian is a leaven in society is passé. To the impatient activist such a man seems out of touch with the pressing needs of today's world.

Lent did not begin as a forty-day season. From earliest church history we know that almost from the beginning there had been a pre-Easter fast, but its duration varied widely from place to place. Some kept one day, some two days, some the forty hours from Good Friday to Easter morning, some three weeks, some six weeks. Gregory the Great, late in the sixth century, established the forty-day period. He had to leave out Sundays, of course, because every Sunday is a feast day in commemoration of Easter. This is why Lent begins on a Wednesday: to make up the forty days without counting the Sundays.

The precedent for the forty-day span was the Lord's fast of similar length in the wildnerness (Matthew 4: 1–11) after his baptism. It has also been pointed out that forty days make up roughly one-tenth of the year, which means that Lent can be regarded as a tithe of one's time.

Gregory spelled out the rule for Lenten fasting. Only one meal a day was allowed, and, said Gregory, "We abstain from flesh, meat, and from all the things that come from flesh, as milk, cheese, and eggs." (For some reason fish was not considered flesh.) The regulations became a matter of state law as well as of church ordinance. In 1570 an English statute set a fine of sixty shillings and a prison term of three months as the penalty for any violation of the Lenten fast. The sick and the infirm could be exempted from fasting if they could get a doctor to certify that they were not able to endure it. This law stayed on the books until 1863, though it had been forgotten many years before.

Lent was not only a time of asking for God's mercy

but also of showing one's own mercy. Money saved by fasting was given in alms. Kings released prisoners and masters freed slaves. Enemies made efforts to be reconciled.

And it was a time of sadness over one's sins. The general tone was penitential. No parties were permitted, and no marriages.

English-speaking peoples are the only ones who use the term "Lent." In the Romance languages the season is called by some form of the word "forty." The German and Dutch terminologies emphasize the fasting aspect.

LITANY. From the Greek *litaneia:* entreaty. A form of prayer in which a leader expresses a series of petitions and the congregation replies to each with a set response. Sometimes the response is simply "Amen" but most frequently it is something more elaborate, such as "Lord, hear our prayer" or "We beseech thee to hear us, good Lord."

Litanies are sometimes sung by the choir and congregation, with the choir and leader in procession and the congregation remaining standing in their pews. There is no reason, however, why the leader and choir must move about; it is perfectly permissible for them to stay in their stalls.

Two litanies appear in the Prayer Book. The one on page 530 is limited to use at Ordinations. The other, on page 54, is titled "The Litany or General Supplication" and may be used at any time, by itself or in connection with Morning Prayer or Evening Prayer or the Holy Communion. Both of these litanies may be either said or sung.

LITURGY. From the Greek *laos:* people, and *ergon:* work. The work of the people, originally any public duty.

101

In the vocabulary of the Church liturgy has two meanings:

(1) All public services. Liturgical worship is common worship in accordance with set forms. In this sense the word is used to draw a distinction between services that follow a formal order and those in some churches that seem to be made up as they go along.

(2) The Eucharist. The sacrament of Holy Communion is often called "the Liturgy" because it is the Church's chief act of public worship.

LOCUM TENENS. From the Latin *locus:* place, and *tenere:* to hold. A temporary deputy. In the Church, a clergyman occupying a cure during a vacancy or an emergency.

LORD'S SUPPER, THE. One of the titles for the sacrament of Christ's Body and Blood. In fact, it is the first of the two titles given in the Prayer Book, on page 67, and would therefore seem to be the Church's preference. In the Prayer Book of 1549 the heading read "The Supper of the Lord, and the Holy Communion, commonly called the Mass." It was changed to its present form in 1552.

"Lord's Supper" was popular among the Puritans and still is the title most used by some Protestant denominations. Each of the names of the sacrament has its own special emphasis. (See EUCHARIST, MASS, HOLY COMMUNION) This one seems to stress the idea that it is primarily a sacred meal of fellowship, which to some minds suggests a memorial repast rather than a sacrament.

LOW SUNDAY. The first Sunday after Easter, probably so called in contrast to the "high" feast of Easter Day. Some wags like to insist that the name refers to the low attendance at church services on this anticlimactic Sunday.

MASS. One of several names for the service of Holy Communion. It probably comes from the Latin *missa*, meaning sent or dismissed, which indicates that it refers to the dismissal, *Ite missa est*, at the conclusion of the Roman Catholic liturgy. It may seem unusual to take the end of any service as a title for the whole, but this is the generally accepted theory about where the term comes from.

The sacrament has several aspects. It is a thanksgiving, a memorial, a statement of unity between God and man and between man and man. It is a common meal, and it is a repleading of the sacrifice on Calvary. No one title can encompass all these meanings. Probably this is why Anglicans use various names at various times.

Episcopalians who talk about "the Mass" (and there are many of them) are likely to be suspected of Roman leanings. Yet, there are also Episcopalians who do not hesitate to call a Christmas Eve or New Year's Eve celebration of the Holy Communion a "Midnight Mass," as if the word "midnight" somehow modified the stigma. It is probably these same semantically sensitive people who would never come right out and call a clergyman a priest but can manage to call him "a priest of the Church."

"Mass" is not an Anglican word, and it will not come easily off the majority of Anglican tongues or strike comfortably against Anglican ears for perhaps another generation or two.

MATRIMONY. From the Latin *mater:* mother, and the Latin suffix *mony*, which denotes a condition or a result. Literally, then, matrimony is the condition of motherhood, which does not come very close to describing what the Church says about it. A condition, yes—but there is much more than motherhood involved.

The old saying, "Marriages are made in heaven," is a good place to start an explanation of the Church's view. Two people find that there exists between them a relationship that is obviously not entirely of their own making. It sounds sentimental to anyone who is not in love, but it would be difficult to convince anyone who is that some outside power did not have a hand in it. They record the situation with the legal authorities; they call their friends and neighbors together to hear them make public acknowledgment of it; and they ask the Church to bless, or "solemnize" it. Neither the state nor the witnesses nor the Church marry them. They enter, the Church says, into a "holy estate," and they do this by their own action. They pledge themselves to live in this heaven-sent relationship, to nourish it, and to work at maintaining it until death ends it.

That is the Church's idea of matrimony: a holy estate, in which two persons have been set apart to live together under these lifelong promises.

MAUNDY THURSDAY. See under HOLY WEEK.

MEMBER. The qualifications for being a member of the Church are not the same as those requried for communicant status. See under COMMUNICANT.

According to Title II, Canon I, "Of the Due Celebration of Sundays," "All persons within this Church shall celebrate and keep the Lord's Day, commonly called Sunday, by regular participation in the public worship of the Church, by hearing the Word of God read and taught, and by other acts of devotion and works of charity, using all godly and sober conversation."

Title I, Canon 16, Section 2, says that if you have fulfilled this requirement over the preceding year you are a member in good standing—not a communicant, just a member.

The language of this canon would drive any good lawyer around the bend. What is "regular"? Once a month? Every three months? What are "other acts of devotion and works of charity"?

The canon does not specify what date that "preceding year" precedes. Is the year the calendar year? Is it the Church year? Is it simply a period of one year before the day when the question of your "good standing" arises? Is it the year preceding the Annual Parish Meeting, when your eligibility to vote may be dubious? One cannot tell by reading the canon.

Nor, surprisingly, is anything said about responsibility for supporting the Church financially. Diocesan canons frequently make up for this omission.

MENSA. A Latin word meaning "table." The top of the altar, or more especially a flat stone set in the top of all Roman and some Anglican altars, on which the sacred vessels are placed at the Eucharist.

METROPOLITAN. A sort of archbishop without the title. This office existed before that of archbishop. The Church, as it grew, created provinces, each consisting of a number of dioceses and usually conforming to the political divisions of the country. The head bishop was appointed for each province and was called the metropolitan, probably because he was usually the bishop of the biggest city—the metropolis—of the province.

He was the chief administrator of his area. The other bishops in his jurisdiction rendered obedience to him and were subject to discipline by him.

For a while after the introduction of archbishops the distinction was made that an archbishop was concerned mainly with spiritual matters while a metropolitan concentrated more on temporalities. Such a division of work was bound to be blurred and artificial. Anglicanism has never recognized it. For example, the Archbishops of Canterbury and York both carry the three titles of metropolitan, archbishop, and primate.

In the American church we do not have metropolitans, although the presidents of our nine provinces are ranked as such in international Anglican meetings, e.g. the Anglican Congress.

See PROVINCE.

MINISTER. From the Latin *minister:* a servant. In general, an agent, one who acts under the orders or authority of someone else.

In the widest sense, all Christians are ministers, agents of God, but traditionally when we use the word we are thinking of a person who, by ordination, is authorized to administer the sacraments, conduct services of worship, preach the Gospel, and be a pastor to the people committed to his care.

The Prayer Book, on pages 294 and 529, makes the statement that there are and have been since the earliest times three categories of ministers in the Church: bishops, priests, and deacons. The Office of Instruction on page 294 spells out the privileges and duties of each echelon.

For many years Episcopalians had trouble making themselves say the word "priest." They were just not comfortable with it, probably a carry-over from the "No Popery" attitude of seventeenth-century England. They talked easily about bishops and deacons, but when it came to priests they almost unanimously called them ministers. The Office of Instruction might as well have said the three orders of the ministry were bishops, ministers, and deacons. Happily, this squeamishness seems to be on the wane.

In the conduct of public worship the Prayer Book unquestionably accepts lay readers as ministers except for those functions that canonically require a priest or bishop. Look, for example, at the rubrics in Morning Prayer. Only the one at the top of page 7, which deals with the Declaration of Absolution, or Remission of Sins, uses the word "priest." All the other directions are for "the Minister," which in this context is intended to include a lay reader.

MINISTRY. Service, aid. In the vocabulary of the Church this word has several meanings beyond its basic one.

Sometimes the entire ordained personnel of the Church is called the ministry. A man who is preparing to become a clergyman is said to be "going into the ministry." In this connotation "the ministry" is the whole body of clergy, collectively—everyone in Holy Orders.

Or "ministry" may mean action. In this sense it is used in two ways:

(1) to describe an individual clergyman's act or acts of service to some person or persons;

(2) to denote the whole Church's care of its own people and its concern for the world outside its membership.

And sometimes the ministry is spoken of as a career

or profession. It may be said of one man that "he went into the ministry" as it would of another that he went into the law, or teaching, or farming.

Even though "ministry" does have these various definitions, it is seldom difficult in any specific instance to recognize the sense in which the term is being used.

MISSAL. The "Mass Book." This is the book on the altar from which the priest reads when he celebrates the Eucharist. Everything in it is from the Book of Common Prayer. In it, besides the service of Holy Communion, with the Collects, Epistles, and Gospels for the whole year, are prayers from the Prayer Book, pages 35 to 53 and 594 to 599.

MISSION. From the Latin *mittere:* to send or let go. The word has at least two meanings in the Church's vocabulary.

The most important definition of it is that it is the Church's business. The Christian Church exists for no other purpose than to "teach all nations, baptizing them in the name of the Father, and of the Son, and of the Holy Ghost" (Matthew 28: 19). One big difficulty here is that it is so easy to read this order as "teach all *other* nations," and thus turn mission into overseas mission. Overseas missions are part of the Lord's command, but only part. The people of Manhattan Island are just as much in need of the Good News as the people of the Fiji Islands, and it is the Church's job to get it to both places. To the extent that she does that she is fulfilling her mission.

Whom does the Church "send" or "let go" to Manhattan or Fiji? Missionaries, we say, and as we say it we picture priests, doctors, teachers, agriculturists, etc., who drop everything else and devote their full time to churches, hospitals, and so on in the inner city or in some jungle clearing. Here again, that is only part of it. Every day the Lord sends you and me, too, into a sick world to represent him—that is, to re-present him—according to our abilities and opportunities. To the extent that we do that we are all missionaries. If we don't do it we are not even Christians.

The secondary meaning of the word "mission" is a church or congregation that is not able, because of its size or perhaps because of its location, to pay its own way and is dependent on the diocese or some other outside source for financial support.

MISSIONARY. See under MISSION.

MONASTERY. From the Greek *monazein:* to live alone. The house of a religious community. There is no authoritative ground for restricting "monastery" to a house for males and calling a house of nuns a "convent." Monastery means the building in which a community of either sex lives.

MONK. A word of uncertain origin, popularly applied to any member of a religious community for men living under vows of poverty, chastity, and obedience. Properly the term is confined to those who actually live in communities and should not be used for associate members who remain in secular society.

MOTHERING SUNDAY. The Fourth Sunday in Lent. It gets its name from the day's Epistle, Galatians 4: 21–31, in which St. Paul writes about the mothers of Abraham's two sons and about "Jerusalem . . . which is the mother of us all."

In medieval England servants were given the day off to be with their mothers. Sons and daughters who had moved away travelled what sometimes amounted to great distances just to spend the day back at their childhood homes. It was the original Mother's Day.

The day is also sometimes called Refreshment Sunday, because the Gospel, from St. John's sixth chapter, is about the miraculous feeding of the five thousand.

MOVABLE FEAST. Any church festival that does not fall on a fixed calendar day but varies in date from year to year.

Easter is the most important of the movable feasts. It may be on any date from March 22 to April 25. Ascension Day and Whitsunday are determined in relation to Easter. So are the beginning of Lent and all the special days within Lent: Passion Sunday, Palm Sunday, Good Friday, etc.

The beginning of the Advent Season is also movable. It depends on Christmas, which, although it is always December 25, falls on various days of the week, and since Advent has to have four Sundays the season may begin on the last Sunday in November or the first in December. The rule is that Advent starts on the Sunday nearest November 30, which is always the fourth Sunday before Christmas.

NARTHEX. A Greek word, brought over into English without change. The narthex in a church building is an anteroom between the front door and the nave. It is the foyer-like space that is often called the "vestibule." Of course, it *is* a vestibule, but narthex is the right word for it when it is in a church.

Depending on the size and grandeur of the building

itself, the narthex may be big and imposing or small and merely utilitarian. And many a church has no narthex at all.

NAVE. Probably from the Latin *navis:* ship. The nave is that part of the church building between the narthex (q.v.) and the chancel (q.v.), or between the front door and the chancel if there is no narthex. It is the area assigned to the laity.

The idea that its name comes from *navis*, which is by no means certain, inspired some poetic soul long ago to suggest that the nave represents the ship of salvation, a charming metaphor although it does carry the implication that the clergy and choir, who are not in the nave, will have to find some other means of transportation to heaven.

There is a chance that nave is a corruption of the Greek *naos:* temple. Compared with the ship image that would be disappointingly dull, but it may be a fact.

Wherever the word may come from, the nave is the part of the church the congregation occupies during services of worship.

NICENE CREED, THE. The first Council of Nicea, in 325, produced a relatively short creed, aimed chiefly at combatting a heresy called Arianism, which was current at the time. Arianism denied the true divinity of Christ and said he was created by the Father. The new creed stated unequivocally that he was truly and eternally God. It ended somewhat abruptly with the words "And in the Holy Spirit," and then tacked on four condemnations of Arianism.

Our present Nicene Creed consists of that original text minus the denunciations of Arianism and plus a good many additions. The section about Jesus has been made considerably longer and more detailed;

111

the former simple mention of the Holy Spirit is now an extended statement of the Spirit's status* and work; and entirely new assertions of belief in the Church, Baptism, the Resurrection of the Dead, and Eternal Life have been introduced.

Credit for the revisions and additions is traditionally given to the Council of Constantinople, which met in 381, but scholars are reluctant to accept this attribution. One reason they hesitate is that they cannot find any testimony earlier than the middle of the fifth century to indicate that Constantinople did it. They do not believe it would take three-quarters of a century for the word about such an important action to get around. They are made still more dubious by the fact that the Nicene Creed was not used in services of worship until around 480.

It would be nice to know the Nicene Creed's authorship and date, but the more important thing about this creed is that it stands as the authoritative statement of Christian belief in both the Eastern and Western parts of the Church.

NOVICE.   From the Latin *novus:* new. A probationary member of a religious community. The period of probation is usually one year. During this time the novice wears the habit and conforms to the rule of the community.

---

* Note that in the statement about the Holy Ghost there is a comma between "the Lord" and "Giver of Life." This is important, but most people saying the creed slide right over it, as if it were "Lord and Giver."

The creed is making two points here:
(1) that the Holy Ghost is God; he is the Lord, co-equal with the Father and the Son, and not a Spirit that derives from the first two Persons of the Trinity,
(2) that he is the Giver of Life.

If you ignore the comma you miss the true meaning of what you are saying.

He or she may be dismissed at any stage during this year or may voluntarily withdraw.

NUN. From the Latin *nonna:* feminine form of *nonnus:* monk. A member of a religious order for women, living under vows of poverty, chastity, and obedience.

OBLATION. From the Latin *oblatus:* offering. Any offering is an oblation but you will seldom hear the word except in connection with ritualistic offerings.

Oblations used to mean all gifts presented by the people at the Eucharist for the use of the clergy, the sick, the poor, the parish, etc. Now the meaning has been narrowed down to refer particularly to the bread and wine to be consecrated for the sacrament.

In earlier times the people brought the bread and wine and gave it to the priest at the offertory. Many parishes are now symbolically reviving this old custom by having parishioners bring bread and wine up the aisle along with the ushers who bring the money. Bread, wine, and money are all oblations, though the Prayer for the whole state of Christ's Church, Prayer Book, page 74, seems to make a distinction between the money on the one hand and the bread and wine on the other by asking God to receive "our alms and oblations."

OFFERTORY. Many people seem to think offertory and offering mean the same thing. They speak of "taking up the offertory."

The offering of money is only part of the offertory. It also includes the offering of the bread and wine that are to be consecrated if the service is Holy Communion. (The priest usually makes this offering for the people but many parishes are reviving the ancient custom of having laypeople bring the bread and wine to the altar.)

The sentence the priest says before the offering is received is part of the offertory. So, too, are the anthem, if one is sung, and the doxology or other ascription that accompanies the presentation.

The offering is what is offered: bread, wine, money. The offertory is the whole ceremony surrounding and including the offering.

OFFICE. (1) A liturgical service. Morning and Evening Prayer are the "daily offices." The Prayer Book services from page 273 to page 342 are called "occasional offices," because they are not used regularly but only when there is occasion for them.

The word "office" is also applied to the eight daily services required to be said by all Roman Catholic clergy and all persons in religious orders. The eight are Matins, Lauds, Prime, Terce, Sext, Nones, Vespers, and Compline.

At the Reformation the Anglican church reduced the eight daily offices to two: Morning Prayer and Evening Prayer. Compline, however, is often still used as a separate service at church conferences, camps, etc.

(2) A position of special responsibility and authority, such as, in the Church, the office of a bishop or the office of a priest. The word appears in this sense in the New Testament several times, the most frequently

quoted of which is I Timothy 3: 1: "If a man desire the office of a bishop, he desireth a good work."

We are familiar with the term in secular usage, from the office of President to the office of dog catcher. People who occupy these special positions in an organization are called officers; in politics they are more often called office-holders. Just what the distinction is, is not clear, but one senses a little more esteem for officers than for office-holders.

OMNISCIENCE. From the Latin *omni:* all, and *scire*: to know. Theologically, omniscience is the attribution to God of all knowledge, the belief that he knows everything past, present, and future.

People who object to the idea that he knows the future do so because they say it negates free will. If God knows what I am going to do, then my choices are only specious choices. My conduct is, in effect, foreordained. I don't really have an option at all.

This argument will not wash. Your best friend may know you so well that he knows what you will do in a given situation, but that does not mean that you have to do it. You could choose to do something else. He just knew you wouldn't.

ORDERS. See HOLY ORDERS.

ORDINAL. The form for the ordination into any or all three of the orders of the ministry. Originally published separately from the other service books, since nobody but a bishop had any need for it, it was bound together with all the other services in the 1549 English Prayer Book and has continued to have a place in the Prayer Book in all subsequent editions.

Our Ordinal, titled "The Form and Manner of Making, Ordaining, and Consecrating Bishops, Priests, and Deacons" is a section of our Prayer Book running from page 529 to page 562.

ORDINAND. A person who is being ordained to one of the three orders of the ministry. In our Ordinal a distinction seems to be made between bishops on the one hand and priests and deacons on the other. The person being ordained a bishop is called in the rubrics "the elected Bishop" or "the Bishop-elect," while the others are called ordinands. But the bishop-elect is still an ordinand just the same.

ORDINARY. In ecclesiastical parlance this word is not the adjective we use in describing something typical or commonplace; it is a noun, a title given to the man who, in a defined geographical area, has the last word on what shall be taught, what rites, customs, or even prayers are permissible in the churches, how disputes are to be settled, and in general how things are to be run in his territory.

When we talk about "the Ordinary" we take for granted that we are referring to the bishop. Nowhere, however, either in the Prayer Book or in the Constitution and Canons of the Church, is the term precisely defined, and *The Oxford Dictionary of the Christian Church* says there are times when it could be understood as meaning the archdeacon.

ORDINATION. From the Latin *ordo:* order. The ceremony in which an individual is commissioned and empowered for the work of the ministry.

The first mention of such formal authorization is in Matthew 10: 1 (the same incident is recorded in Mark 3: 14 and 15), which tells that Jesus "called to him his twelve disciples and gave them authority over unclean spirits, to cast them out, and to heal every disease and every infirmity."

The commitment of a far more extensive power is described in John 20: 21–23, when Jesus, after his resurrection, breathed on the Apostles and said to them, "As my Father hath sent me, even so send I you," and gave them the ability to forgive or retain sins. It is this passage from St. John's Gospel that furnishes the pattern for ordinations in the Episcopal Church. In the Ordering of Priests and the Consecration of Bishops the opening words of the empowering formula are "Receive the Holy Ghost," and the Ordering of Priests also quotes from St. John the words, "Whose sins thou dost forgive, they are forgiven; and whose sins thou dost retain, they are retained." The Spirit is transmitted by the laying of hands on the ordinand's head, rather than by breathing on him. To this extent the present form varies from the scriptural one.

The power to ordain is limited to bishops, as successors and heirs of the Apostles, to whom the gift was originally given. In the Ordering of Priests, however, the other priests present are directed by rubric to lay their hands, along with the bishop's, on the ordinand's head.

It takes only one bishop to consecrate another one, but the Church traditionally requires three. This is not a theological matter; rather it is a practical safeguard left over from the times when the credentials of some bishops were open to doubt. With three consecrators it seems fairly certain that at least one will be qualified.

ORIGINAL SIN. The general cussedness that is in all of us. We seem to be born with it.

The Jews tried to account for it by saying we inherit it from Adam and Eve, who got it by eating the fruit of the tree of knowledge of good and evil (Genesis, chapter 3). Today we would be more likely to describe

117

it as the inherent conflict between the instinct of self-preservation and the instinct of race-preservation. However you explain it, we all know we have it.

Calvinists, in their Westminster Confession, said man is "utterly corrupt." Anglicans do not go that far. Article 9 of our Articles of Religion (q.v.) says man is "very far gone from original righteousness," which is certainly not the same thing as being completely depraved.

The Article (Prayer Book, page 604) goes on to expound Original Sin as an ambivalence in man which makes "the flesh lust always contrary to the Spirit," and says this inclination toward evil is an "infection of nature" that remains even "in them that are regenerated."

The saints have always acknowledged the presence in themselves of this pull away from righteousness. Sentimental humanists since the 1920's, however, have denied that it is an inborn condition in mankind. They believe that with more education and better laws man can become perfect. He was born good but was later corrupted by the evil environment created by adults who, presumably, were born good but later corrupted by the evil environment created by adults, who, etc., etc., way back to some point in the dim, misty past when a generation of perfect babies without any naughty environment to seduce them, spontaneously turned into a generation of wicked adults and established a corruptive pattern for all succeeding generations.

St. Paul states the opposite view succinctly: "The good that I would, I do not: but the evil which I would not, that I do" (Romans 7: 19). If we are honest, that strikes a responsive note in every one of us.

If this were the whole story it would put us all in a hopeless predicament. But Christianity does not leave it there. Article 9 also says that "there is no condemnation for them that believe and are baptized." Salvation does not depend on what we do or don't do. We are saved by our acceptance of and union with Christ, not by our merits or works.

Original Sin was what the Psalmist had in mind when he wrote "In sin did my mother conceive me." (Psalm 51: 5) Many are shocked at this passage because they think it means the reproductive process by which children are conceived is sinful. It doesn't mean that at all. The Psalmist is saying that he finds sin so deep in his nature that he knows it must have been in him since the moment of his conception.

The dogma of the Immaculate Conception of the Blessed Virgin Mary, belief in which is required of Roman Catholics but not of Anglicans, is the other side of the same coin. Theologians started with the belief that Mary was without Original Sin. The question then arose, "When did she lose it?" And the only possible answer was that she never had it. She was conceived without it.

OXFORD MOVEMENT. This was an early-nineteenth-century movement, centered at Oxford University, aimed at reawakening the Church of England to the Catholic aspects of its heritage.

The Church of England was in pretty bad shape in those days. Extreme liberals were running both the religion and the government of the country—Church and State were one. And the liberals were not just Protestants gone wild: they were militant anti-religionists. They wanted to get rid of the creeds; they wanted to remove from the Prayer Book all mention of the Holy Trinity. They denied that there is regeneration in Baptism; they denied that a priest has power to absolve sins. If they had been able to reform the Anglican Church according to their theology, or lack of theology, there wouldn't have been much left of it.

The people were apathetic. On Easter Day in 1809, at St. Paul's Cathedral in London, only nine persons made their communions.

That's the way things were when, on July 14, 1833, John Keble climbed into one of the pulpits in Oxford and preached a scorcher entitled "National Apostasy," that is, national desertion of the Faith. This sermon is usually regarded as the beginning of the Oxford Movement. Actually, of course, it was only the Movement's emergence into the open. Indignation and alarm had been brewing for a long time among a group at Oxford whose leaders, besides Keble, were John Henry Newman and Edward Bouverie Pusey, and whose names will forever light up Anglican church history.

These men hammered away at three main points: (1) that the Church of England is a branch of the Church founded by Jesus himself, (2) that its clergy are in the Apostolic Succession (q.v.); and (3) that the Book of Common Prayer is the Church of England's rule of faith.

But these basics had inescapable implications. You can't espouse them without taking the next step and believing (1) the Real Presence of Christ in the Eucharist and (2) the essential independence of Church from State. It was all too much for the liberal party.

In spite of all the screaming from press, government, and liberal clergy, the Movement spread rapidly. It met the desperate needs of an impoverished church.

Inevitable by-products were a re-introduction of ancient ceremony into the services of worship, an emphasis on the dignity and responsibility of the clergy, and the revival of religious communities for men and women. These, too, angered the Movement's opponents.

Now, a century and a half later, it is impossible to measure our debt to this handful of fiercely devoted men who by their endurance in the face of scorn and staggering odds revitalized Anglicanism both in England and around the world.

Look where you will in your own parish church. Crosses, candles, pictures, vestments give a beauty to your church and its services that couldn't be there if these few had not stirred our entire Communion to an awareness of its Catholic character. They took the drabness out of worship.

But far more important than any aesthetic adornments we may enjoy is the doctrinal difference their influence has made. Thanks to them we know again what we forgot for centuries: that we are the Church, the Holy Catholic Universal Apostolic Church in all its grandeur, and not just a little group of like-minded people who got together because they subscribed to some one man's presentation of the Christian faith, or part of it.

The Oxford Movement is not to be confused with the Oxford Group Movement, which was started in Oxford in the 1920s by Frank N. D. Buchman, flourished worldwide in the 1930s, and is still going under the name of Moral Rearmament.

PALL. From the Latin *pallium:* a long white garment worn by Roman women. In church parlance the word is applied to two kinds of cloth covering:

(1) The linen cloth with which the chalice is cov-

ered at the Eucharist. This is a small piece of a square of material stiffened by cardboard or sometimes a square of glass inserted into it from one side. It is difficult to see any connection between this scrap of linen and a Roman lady's dress.

(2) A large cloth, usually of black, purple, or white velvet or lined silk, which is spread over the coffin at a funeral.

PALM SUNDAY. See under HOLY WEEK.

PARISH. From the Greek *paroikia:* neighborhood. In its original sense a parish is a geographical area. Ask an English parson how many people he has in his parish and he will say 25,000 or some such astounding figure. He counts everybody who lives within the bounds of his strictly defined territory, his "neighborhood."

We Americans are more realistic about it. We count only communicants and baptized persons as members of our parishes. Theoretically, perhaps, we may think of a parish as an area, but practically we treat it as a group of communicants and baptized persons that is able to sustain financial self-sufficiency. The determinant is this matter of self-support. If the organized unit can pay its own way, the diocese admits it to parish status; if it can't it remains a mission (q.v.) until it can.

The geographical idea of a parish still holds on in some dioceses—Virginia, for example. The boundaries there are clear, at least on the map. That goes back to the time when Virginia was made up of rural communities. But it won't work in our modern urban situations. How could Manhattan Island be cut up into geographical parochial units? Trinity Parish there has five chapels besides the parish church at the head of

122

Wall Street, and they are scattered all over Manhattan. Any boundaries you tried to fix for Trinity Parish would cross the boundaries of other parishes from one end of the island to the other.

So, to us in America at least, the practical working definition of a parish is a congregation that supports itself.

PARISH HOUSE. The unconsecrated building or part of a building in the church "plant." The section apart from the church proper, used for offices, classrooms, recreation, dinners, etc.

PARISH MEETING, ANNUAL. Every diocese has its canons that spell out precisely when, where, and how vestries are elected. They tell who can vote on such occasions, how many electors are needed to make a quorum, who can be elected, and how long the vestryman's term runs. They all require such meetings to be held once a year.

The national canons have little to say on the subject. They recognize the need for vestrymen, but they leave the method of getting them up to the diocesan canons and the state law.

The only definitely declared purpose of the Annual Parish Meeting is to elect vestrymen.

Not a parish in the country has been satisfied to leave it at that. Over the years so many extraneous items have crept into the agenda of the average parish meeting that it has become without any doubt the dullest interlude in the annual cycle of parish life.

There are reports from the Church School, the women's guilds, the choir, Boy Scouts, Girl Scouts —any and all organizations in any way associated with the parish. Nobody listens to these, but people do perk up a bit when the treasurer reveals the financial situation. Then the rector exaggerates the number of

123

calls he has made during the past year, tells how many persons he has baptized, presented for Confirmation, married, buried, received by transfer and transferred out, and gives his blessing and lets everybody go.

A quorum for an Annual Parish Meeting is always low, sometimes as low as five eligible voters. Even so it is often hard to get a quorum.

PARISH RECORDS. The national canons require that every "Minister of this Church" (that would mean vicars and priests-in-charge as well as rectors) record in the parish register all Baptisms, Confirmations, Marriages, Burials, and the names of all communicants within his cure.

He must also indicate those whose names have been removed by letter of transfer, those whose domicile in unknown, and those whose domicile is known but who are inactive.

PARSON. This is simply the Latin *persona:* person, brought over into English and subjected to the same coy national affectation that impels the British to make clark out of clerk and darby out of derby.

It was in the eleventh century that the term was first used. It was a legal word, applied to the rector of a parish because in matters pertaining to the law he was the designated "person" to deal with. All the parish lands and other assets were registered in his name. If you wanted to sue the parish, for instance, you sued him as its official representative.

For many years the term was used only in reference to the rector of a parish. Vicars and assistant priests were not "persons" because they did not have the necessary legal status. Only one man could hold title to the parish property and therefore only one could act for the parish in the courts.

Nowadays any clergyman may be called a parson

without any distinction as to his position in a parish organization. Roman Catholics, however, do not often use the word in connection with their own priests, and bishops seem to be entirely above it. A parson is generally thought of as a clergyman on the local parish level.

PASCHAL CANDLE. A large candle placed in a large candlestick in the north side of the sanctury and lighted at all services throughout Eastertide. It is often extinguished finally after the Gospel on Ascension Day.

Eastertide is also known as the Paschal Season. Paschal comes from Pesach, the Hebrew word for Passover. This is a little confusing, but remember, the first Easter came at the time of the Passover festival, and the early Christians were all Jews, who kept both Easter and Passover.

PASSION SUNDAY. The fifth Sunday in Lent, called Passion Sunday because it is the beginning of Passiontide, the last two weeks in Lent.

PASTOR. A shepherd. The word is the same in both Latin and English.

When we call a clergyman a pastor we are using figurative language to say that his relationship to his lay people is like that of a shepherd to his flock—a caring, tending responsibility. The implication that the people are like sheep doesn't seem to bother anybody.

All Lutheran clergymen are called Pastor. The trouble with this is that it emphasizes one aspect of the man's ministry to the exclusion of the priestly and prophetic.

PATEN. From the Greek *patane:* a shallow vessel.

The plate, usually silver or gold, from which the consecrated bread is administered at the Holy Communion.

"PEEKABOO PRAYER." A feebly funny description of the way the choir prayer is said by some of the clergy. It is a "peekaboo" performance when a priest, having gone out of the nave with the choir, pokes his head back in for the prayer. He wants the congregation to feel that they are participating. In short, he doesn't know what he is doing.

A choir prayer is just what its name indicates: a prayer with and for the choir. The congregation is in no way involved in it. But the Episcopal Church can't bear to end anything. The Prayer Book says the priest "shall let them depart" with the blessing. But nobody pays any attention to that. There has to be a recessional hymn after the blessing. That surely ought to end matters, but No. Everybody has to kneel again for a prayer with a choir that has already left. Is that the end? Not at all. The people must remain kneeling for the solemn snuffing out of the candles. And even then it isn't over. After the candles are out nobody can move until the organ blasts out the opening notes of a postlude. Only then are the faithful set free.

PENTECOST. See WHITSUNDAY.

PEW. The derivation of this word, from the Latin *podium,* seems inept. Everybody knows that a podium is an elevated platform, and that is not what a pew is or ever was.

At first pews in churches were compartments providing seats for families or other groups. Each family or group had its regular pew, for which they paid an annual rent. When pews became straight benches, as most of them are now, the custom of renting them and thus temporarily "owning" them continued. There is hardly any parish left now where the people pay pew-rent, but old habits die hard and in many churches some families are so accustomed to sitting always in the same place that if you blunder into their usual seats you feel like a trespasser.

PISCINA. From the Latin *piscis:* fish, plus *inus:* belonging to. A fish tank or pool. In the church a piscina is a basin, usually in the sacristy, with a drain that empties directly on the ground. Into it is poured the water that has been used in Baptism and in cleansing the Holy Communion vessels and linens.

Our reason for calling this facility a fish tank seems a little obscure.

POSTCOMMUNION. The part of the Eucharist said after the people have received communion.

POSTULANT. A person, male or female, who is going through the preliminary stages of testing before being admitted as a novice in a religious order.

PRAYER BOOK. See BOOK OF COMMON PRAYER.

PREACHER. Our English word "preach" comes from two Latin words: *prae:* before, and *dicare:* to say. A preacher, then, is someone who says something before some kind of audience, presumably a congregation. Experience has taught us that he does not always say something *to* them. "Before" seems to be the right word.

Even though preaching is only one of their many activities, Protestant ministers are commonly called preachers. Anglican clergy do not like to have the term applied to them. The reason they do not like it, they say, is that they are preachers only when they are preaching, which is at most only a few minutes a week. This seems rather a weak demurrer. Writers are writers even though they are not at the moment putting pen to paper; sailors are sailors though they may be in port.

The real objection is not in the realm of semantics. What bothers our clergy is that calling them preachers leaves out at least half the story. In our Catholic concept of the ministry the minister has two main functions: the prophetic and the priestly. He serves both in the pulpit and at the altar. The term "preacher" describes him only as a prophet and ignores his priesthood. This is really why it irritates him, and his remonstrance on this basis is a valid one.

PREFACE. The section of the Eucharist immediately preceding the prayer of consecration. It begins with the Sursum Corda "(Lift up your hearts)" on page 76 of the Prayer Book and ends with the Sanctus "(Holy, Holy, Holy, Lord God of Hosts)" on page 77.

The Prayer Book provides, on pages 78 and 79, special insertions, called Proper Prefaces, for Christmas, Epiphany, Purification, Annunciation, Transfiguration, Easter, Ascension, and Whitsuntide. These are read between the Sursum Corda and the Sanctus.

PRELATE. From the Latin *praelatus:* preferred. Formerly prelates might be church dignitaries of various ranks and functions. In the Anglican Communion the term is now applied chiefly to bishops.

PRESIDING BISHOP. See under BISHOP.

PRIEST. A contraction of the Greek *presbyteros:* elder.

A priest is a member of the second of the three orders of Christian ministers, bishops being the first and deacons the third. The duties of bishops and deacons have been clear from the beginning. The Prayer Book, page 294, spells out just what it is that a priest does: . . . to minister to the people committed to his care; to preach the word of God; to baptize; to celebrate the Holy Communion; and to pronounce Absolution and Blessing in God's name. But his job specifications have not always been so neatly stated.

On page 529 the Prayer Book says there have been bishops, priests, and deacons "from the Apostles' time," and so there have if you are willing to equate the New Testament "elder" with today's "priest." However, it was some time before the elder, or presbyter, was much more than a proxy for the bishop.

PRIMATE. From the Latin *primus:* first. Originally the title of the bishop of the "first see," that is, the ranking diocese of a province. Now, in Anglicanism it is applied to the chief bishop of one of our national churches.

The Archbishop of Canterbury, for example, is Primate of All England, and his diocese is the "Primatial See." In an honorary sort of way he is Primate of the whole Anglican Communion, but he has no real authority outside England.

Some confusion results from the fact that the Archbishop of York is called Primate of England—not "all England," just England. This goes back to the time when Canterbury and York and their two Archbishops engaged in a six-century-long struggle for supremacy. Pope Innocent VI (1352-62) decided that Canterbury should have precedence and gave the two contestants the titles they still have. If Canterbury is Primate of All England it is hard to see how York's "Primate of England" can mean what it says.

Our Presiding Bishop does not have a diocese

but he is nevertheless the Primate of the American church. There are many who think we should have a Primatial See for him, in which he would live and have local responsibility during his tenure as Presiding Bishop.

PROPERS. The Collect, Epistle, and Gospel for the day, as printed in the Book of Common Prayer, pages 90 to 269.

In early times the priest at Holy Communion selected whatever Scripture readings he pleased, and he did not limit himself to two or to the New Testament. Gradually, however, beginning in the fourth century, the tendency was for the Church to prescribe certain passages, having, if possible, something to do with the day, and to limit the number to two—one from the Epistles and one from the Gospels. In a very few instances an Old Testament lesson was appointed for the Epistle. This is still occasionally done—for example, the Epistle for Ash Wednesday is from the book of the Prophet Joel.

The reading of the Gospel lesson has always been attended by special ceremony. From primitive times the people have stood reverently while it is read. Custom has decreed that the Gospel be read by no one below the rank of deacon.

The Collect is not, as many suppose, so called because it sums up or collects the thoughts of the Epistle and Gospel. The Latin *collecta* refers to an assembly, or collection, of people. So the word "collect" as we use it here means the opening prayer of the service for which the people are gathered.

PROPER PREFACE. See under PREFACE.

PROPITIATION. From the Latin *propitius:* favorable. Appeasing the wrath of God—making him favorable—by prayer or sacrifice when one has committed an offense against him.

To the Christian this sounds too much like buying forgiveness, which cannot be done. It wouldn't be forgiveness if it could be bargained for.

God cannot accept a burnt lamb on an altar as paying for a theft or a murder any more than an offended wife can accept a mink coat as a quid pro quo for an act of adultery by her husband.

In any forgiveness the conditions are (1) a genuine repentance on the part of the offender, and (2) a willingness on the part of the offended to live with the pain of the offense rather than let a relationship be broken. The elements are personal ones, not subject to a negotiating process.

PROTESTANT. "Protest" is a tricky word, whether you are talking about a theological position or a political demonstration. It has been maneuvered around into meaning exactly the opposite of what it started out to mean. *Pro* in Latin is "for"; *testare* is "to witness." To protest, therefore, ought to mean to witness *for* something.

Webster doesn't even make a slight bow in the direction of the word's literal definition. He says a protest is "the formal expression of objection or disapproval." And the same with it as a verb. To protest is to object. Completely negative. To witness *against*.

The word "Protestant" was first used in 1529 in reference to the German princes who at the second Diet of Speyer submitted an objection to an edict that threatened to choke off Martin Luther's reform movement. An earlier Diet had voted to allow each prince of the empire to determine whether the religion in his principality should be Catholic or reformed. The second Diet cancelled that permission, whereupon six princes, representing fourteen cities, issued

131

a "protestation." They said, "In matters which concern God's honor and salvation and the eternal life of our souls, everyone must stand and give an account before God for himself."

That was a positive statement, but its purpose was to register opposition, and from that time on the general public, not attuned to semantic subtleties, has regarded protest as disagreement.

The first organized groups to be called Protestants were, naturally, the followers of Martin Luther, whom the six princes had been trying to protect, but by now the term has been applied to all non-Roman groups, from Anglicans to Holy Rollers.

We Americans are the only Anglicans who use the word "Protestant" in the official name of our church. It has never suited us very well, because we are at least as Catholic as we are Protestant.

The basic principles of Protestantism are three. They are all, incidentally, affirmative, not opposed to anything:

(1) The supremacy of the Bible in determining matters of dogma,

(2) The supremacy of grace (q.v.) as the means of man's salvation,

(3) The priesthood of all believers, as contrasted with the limitation of priesthood to a professional caste.

The elements of a Catholic church as laid out in the Lambreth Quadrilateral (q.v.) are:

(1) Belief in the Apostles' and Nicene Creeds,

(2) Belief in the Holy Scriptures,

(3) Continuance in the Apostolic Ministry,

(4) Acceptance of Holy Baptism and the Holy Communion as generally necessary to salvation.

Obviously the latter list describes us better than the

first one. However, we reject doctrinal developments promulgated by Rome that we do not consider adequately grounded in Scriptures or Creeds. We do not think, for example, that one cannot be saved if one doesn't believe in Transubstantiation, the Immaculate Conception and the Assumption of Mary, or the Infallibility of the Pope.

We agree with Rome in believing in the Apostolic Succession, the Real Presence of Christ in the Eucharist, and other matters of doctrine that are repudiated or ignored by leading Protestant bodies. We do not insist on private confession but we do provide it on request. And we hold that a priest has power "to pronounce Absolution and blessing in God's Name." (Prayer Book, page 294)

Certainly we have more in common with the Pope than we have with Billy Graham.

There was nothing very interesting about the way "Protestant" got into the name of the American church. In Colonial times in Maryland, which was almost solidly Roman Catholic, members of the Church of England were generally called Protestant Episcopalians. "Protestant" distinguished them from the Romanist population, and "episcopalian" set them apart from the non-Romans, who didn't have bishops. (Not that the Church of England had any bishops in America—but the episcopate was one of the characteristics of Anglican organization.)

In 1780, when, a little prematurely, three Maryland clergymen and an unrecorded number of laymen held a local convention, they voted to call themselves the Protestant Episcopal Church, not because anyone particularly advocated it but simply because by that time they were used to it.

In 1785 the first General Convention made it official for the whole American church. "Reformed Episcopal" was suggested but got nowhere. The deputies present had heard "Protestant Episcopalian" for so long, most of them probably felt it was already the church's name and they were merely rubber-stamping a *fait accompli.*

For a number of years many people have been trying to get "Protestant" removed because in their view it is inaccurate and misleading, but the best they have been able to do so far is to get General Convention to allow two official names: Protestant Episcopal or just plain Episcopal. This hardly satisfies anyone.

PROVINCE. The Episcopal Church is divided into nine geographical areas called provinces. The numbers and names of the provinces, and the territories included in each of them are as follows:

PROVINCE I	*New England*	The six New England states
PROVINCE II	*New York and New Jersey*	New York, New Jersey, and Haiti
PROVINCE III	*Washington*	Pennsylvania, Delaware, Maryland, Virginia, West Virginia, and the District of Columbia
PROVINCE IV	*Sewanee*	Alabama, North Carolina, South Carolina, Georgia, Florida, Mississippi, Louisiana, Tennessee, and Kentucky
PROVINCE V	*Mid-West*	Ohio, Indiana, Illinois, Wisconsin, and Michigan
PROVINCE VI	*Northwest*	Minnesota, Iowa, Nebraska, Colorado, Wyoming, North Dakota, South Dakota, and Montana
PROVINCE VII	*Southwest*	Missouri, Kansas, Arkansas, Texas, Oklahoma, and New Mexico
PROVINCE VIII	*Pacific*	Arizona, Utah, Idaho,

| | | Nevada, Washington, Oregon, California, Hawaii, Alaska, the Philippines, and Taiwan |
| PROVINCE IX | *Caribbean* | Columbia, Costa Rica, Dominican Republic, Ecuador, El Salvador, Guatemala, Honduras, Mexico, Nicaragua, Puerto Rico, Panama, and the Canal Zone. |

Meetings of the provinces are called Synods. They are in most cases held annually except in General Convention years. The Synod, like the General Convention, consists of two Houses: Bishops and Deputies. The House of Deputies is made up of clergy and laity from the dioceses of the province. Each diocese makes its own decision about how its Deputies are chosen.

Each province has a president, elected by the Synod from among its own bishops for a term fixed by the province. The president presides at Synods and at interim meetings of the bishops as the need arises. He has no power over the other bishops or within their jurisdictions. Technically, however, and by courtesy, he is ranked as an archbishop or metropolitan during his term of office. Our American church is informal and casual about this sort of honor and there is no pomp connected with the office of president of a province. It is only at international meetings of the Anglican Communion that the matter of rank comes up, and on such occasions the provincial presidents are treated as archbishops.

The powers of a province are also negligible. It has, of course, the right to organize and regulate its own Synod. It can originate programs of its own within its boundaries or take on duties or projects assigned to it by General Convention. It can create a budget for its provincial work—and raise the money for it. It can also elect members of the national Executive Council.

The province cannot control the policies or affairs of any of its constituent dioceses, nor can it take any action that conflicts with the national Constitution or Canons.

It is admitted that the provinces as now constituted do not cut much ice in the life or structure of the Church, and there are those who are strongly in favor of abolishing them as a waste of time and money.

On the other side there are those who believe there are constructive values in bringing together the church people of a more or less homogeneous section of the country, if only to discuss their peculiar common problems and exchange ideas.

Perhaps the best reason for retaining the provinces lies in the future. Even now the population growth in America is making General Convention unwieldy. As the two Houses in General Convention grow, the Convention, especially the House of Deputies, is finding its agenda more and more determined by pre-Convention committees, and grassroots concerns less and less represented. It is increasingly difficult for a two-week Convention to give all its constituents a hearing. Many diocesan deputations leave General Convention feeling that they have had no voice in it at all.

It is conceivable that the time may come when the Deputies at General Convention are there as representatives of the provinces rather than of dioceses. This would greatly decrease the number of persons present at General Convention and would therefore not only reduce the parliamentary anonymity of the Convention as it is now necessarily organized, but also greatly increase the interest of the dioceses in their provinces and elevate the importance of the provinces in the national life of the Church.

PSALM. From the Greek *psalmos:* a song.

Every so often some long-time Episcopalian suddenly becomes aware that the Psalms in the Book of Common Prayer are not in quite the same words as those in the King James Bible. This happens most frequently when Psalm 23 is read in church. Some people are startled; some are distressed. It is nothing to get excited about. The first Book of Common Prayer appeared in 1549, sixty-two years before the King James version was completed. Archbishop Thomas Cranmer, the compiler of that first book, had to use what was available.

What was available was the translation by Miles Coverdale, finished in 1535. It had been ordered by King Henry VIII as a result of a petition he had received from the Canterbury Convocation in 1534. To deliver the translation in one year was very quick action on the part of Coverdale. One suspects that he had been at work for some time before he got the order.

The Psalms are Jewish hymns, for which the Hebrew name is Tehillim, "songs of praise." The 150 Psalms now in the Bible formed the hymnal used in the second temple at Jerusalem, which was built late in the sixth century B.C., when the Jews returned from their seventy-year exile in Babylon.

Though their lack of meter or rhyme may deceive us, the Psalms are poetry. In Hebrew they do have a rhythm, but it is lost to us in translation. In the Hebrew poetic scheme each verse falls into two parts. In some verses the second part repeats the first in different words; in others the second part may provide a contrast to the first or supplement it. In the Prayer

137

Book Psalter, an asterisk marks the division within each verse.

The Psalms are frequently called the Psalms of David. In earlier times it was believed that David wrote them all. He may have written a few, but most are the work of other writers, many of them much later than the tenth century B.C., when David lived.

Our custom of adding a Gloria after each Psalm or group of Psalms is designed to bring a Christian element into the otherwise purely Jewish hymns.

PSALTER. From the Greek *psalterion,* a stringed instrument much like a zither. In English the word for the instrument is psaltery. "Praise him with the sound of the trumpet, praise him with the psaltery and harp" (Psalm 140:3). The clear indication here is that psalms are to be sung.

In common usage today the word "Psalter" means simply the whole collection of Psalms, all 150 of them.

The Psalms are often printed in a book by themselves, separate from the rest of the Bible. Such a book, too, is called a Psalter. So also is the section of the Book of Common Prayer, in which the Psalms are arranged for liturgical or devotional use.

PULPIT. From the Latin *pulpitum:* a stage or scaffold. An elevated stand of wood or stone where the preacher stands. Sometimes pulpits are elaborately carved and decorated; sometimes they are quite plain. How fancy the pulpit is will depend largely on the elegance of the whole church.

Pulpits are not ancient in the church. They came into use in the late Middle Ages. Before that bishops preached from their chairs, others from a simple platform called an ambo.

The north side of the nave is considered by many to be the proper place for the pulpit, but there is no general agreement on the matter.

138

PURIFICATOR. From the Latin *purus:* pure, plus *facere:* to make. A small piece of white linen used at the Holy Communion to cleanse the chalice. Some priests wipe the rim of the chalice after each person drinks from it; others use the purificator only after all have made their communion.

PYX. From the Greek *pyxis:* a wooden box. In the Christian Church a pyx was at first any receptacle used to contain the consecrated bread of the Blessed Sacrament when it was reserved for use between celebrations of the Holy Communion. Now the term is applied to (1) a small flat gold or silver box in which the Sacrament is carried to the sick, or (2) a larger vessel in which the consecrated bread is kept in the tabernacle on the altar.

In some churches, where there is no tabernacle, they have a "hanging pyx." This is a gold or silver container hung from a wall bracket near the altar or from the ceiling.

REAL PRESENCE, THE. A distinctively Anglican doctrine that emphasizes the actual presence of the Body and Blood of Christ in the Eucharist. This is in contrast with those theologies that hold that the Body and Blood are present only figuratively or symbolically.

The doctrine of the Real Presence does, however, stop short of the Roman Catholic attempt (Transubstantiation) to define explicitly how the mystical phenomenon occurs.

RECTOR. From the Latin *regere:* to rule. In the American church a rector is a priest who is the chief clergyman over a self-supporting congregation. "Ruler" is a strong word, and how much actual ruling he can do usually depends on his own tact and the cooperation of his people. But the canons do give him a lot of power.

Parishes (q.v.) have rectors; missions (q.v.) have vicars. The only determinant is whether the church pays its own way or gets help from the diocese.

A parish may have several clergymen but it can have only one rector. The others are assistants on the rector's staff. Sometimes an assistant priest is called an associate rector. This sounds important but it doesn't mean a thing. No matter what titles you give them, all the clergy on the staff are still assistants.

Sometimes a newspaper will report that a man was ordained rector. Such a statement comes either from ignorance or from an abhorrence of the word "priest." Nobody was ever ordained rector. Bishops, priests, and deacons are ordained to be bishops, priests, and deacons of the whole Church. A rector is a priest who is elected by the vestry of one parish to be the "ruler" of that particular parish.

RECTORY. The house, usually supplied by the parish in which the rector lives. Roman Catholics use the same word; Protestants in general call their pastor's house a parsonage, though Presbyterians call it the manse—short for mansion.

Newspaper writers and other uninformed persons often say "parish house" (q.v.) when they mean rectory.

RED LETTER DAYS. A term once used for the more important festivals and saints' days of the year. Nowadays church calendars are printed in the seasonal colors: Christmas and Easter in white, Pentecost in red. In earlier times only red and black were used in the calendar, and red was the color of the days regarded as especially significant.

This is an expression that has come from the church vocabulary into everyday speech. A red letter day now means some gala occasion in the life of an individual or a community. Many people use the term today without having any idea where it came from.

RELIGIOUS. As a noun this is a technical term for a member of a monastic or "religious" order, whether a priest, layman, or laywoman. The English language has an incorrigible tendency to turn adjectives into nouns—an evening dress is a "formal," the armed forces are the "military," an automobile whose top can be put up and down is a "convertible,"—and this is only another example of that tendency.

Also, the use of the term "a religious" to mean a member of an order is, by implication, restrictive. It seems to say that if you don't belong to an order you are not religious.

A priest who is not "a religious" is called a secular priest. Why he is not called just "a secular" is not clear, but it is something to be thankful for.

RELIGIOUS ORDER. A segregated community of monks, friars, or nuns living under vows of poverty, chastity, and obedience, and, usually, wearing a distinctive garb, called a habit.

The degree of segregation ranges from complete withdrawal from the outside world to just living communally while maintaining normal contacts through teaching, preaching, slum work, missionary work, etc. Those that cut themselves off entirely from society are called "cloistered orders."

In the Anglican Communion the revival of religious

orders, which had been non-existent since the Reformation, was one of the fruits of the Oxford Movement (q.v.).

The Episcopal Church now has about twelve orders for men and a similar number for women. Some of them do not require that their members live in community but only that they live under the order's rule of discipline wherever they are.

REREDOS. A curiously jumbled Anglicization of three Latin words: *ad:* to; *retro:* backward; and *dos:* back. "Backward to the back"—it is hard to see how a word could hold much more redundancy than that.

The term has various meanings, but in church a reredos is any decoration put up behind an altar.

The earliest type was a painting of a scene or a symbol on the wall against which the altar stood. Later on it might be a silken hanging (see also DOSSAL) or a piece of jewelled metal-work.

In these times a reredos may also be a mural or a painted wooden panel behind the altar. Or it may be a carving, in wood, stone, or alabaster. The paintings or carvings usually represent biblical incidents or figures of saints.

RESERVED SACRAMENT. Consecrated bread (and sometimes wine) kept in the church, originally, and still primarily, for the Communion of the Sick. It may be housed in a tabernacle (q.v.), in a hanging pyx (q.v.), or in an aumbry (q.v.) in the wall. In cases of accidents or sudden seizures the fact that this bread has already been consecrated saves the priest a considerable amount of time in getting it to the stricken person.

The practice of reservation is referred to in Christian writings as early as the second century. It was forbidden in England at the time of the Reformation and only in recent years has been revived on any sizable scale.

There are many people who find a special spiritual benefit in praying before an altar where the Sacrament is reserved. Article XXVIII of the Articles of Religion, Prayer Book, page 608, seems, on one interpretation, to prohibit reservation for this or any other purpose. It says, "The Sacrament of the Lord's Supper was not by Christ's ordinance reserved, carried about, lifted up, or worshipped." Those who value the presence of the Reserved Sacrament say the Article is irrelevant. In the first place they do not worship it, and in the second place nobody ever claimed it was reserved "by Christ's ordinance."

RETABLE.   A shelf behind the altar on which the cross, candlesticks, and other ornaments may be placed. Its proper name is "gradine," from the Latin *gradus:* a step, but hardly anyone calls it that.

REVEREND.   From the Latin *revereri:* worthy of reverence.

This is one of the most misused words in the English language. It is an adjective, but most people use it as a noun. In fact, many people even apologize when they fail to misuse it. They will say, "Mr. Smith. Oh, I beg your pardon, I mean Reverend Smith."

Reverend is not a noun-title, like Captain or President or Judge. It is rather a description, like Honorable, given in courtesy to clergymen, just as the term Honorable is by courtesy prefixed to the names of certain political office-holders.

It is just as wrong to say "Good morning, Reverend" to a clergyman as it would be to say "Good morning, Honorable" to the mayor. It is just as wrong to call a clergyman "Reverend Smith" as it would be to call a mayor "Honorable Smith."

"Reverend" is no different from any other adjective. The proper way to greet a clergyman is "Good morning, Mr. (or Father or Doctor) Smith." Referring to him or addressing a letter to him, you say or write "The Reverend Mr." or "The Rev. John Smith."

Sometimes someone who has partly gotten the idea will talk about "the Reverend Smith." Or a newspaper, thinking it is avoiding the usual colloquialism, will group several clergymen as "the Revs. Smith, Jones, and Brown." Just putting "the" in doesn't make it correct. It has to be "the Rev. Mr. Smith," "the Rev. Messrs. Smith, Jones, and Brown."

ROGATION. From the Latin *rogare:* to ask or to pray. In this case to pray especially for the coming season's crops. The fifth Sunday after Easter is, as the Prayer Book, page 175, says, "commonly called Rogation Sunday." The Monday, Tuesday, and Wednesday following are Rogation Days.

Little is done about Rogation Sunday and almost nothing about the three Rogation Days now, but in rural England a few centuries ago, when everyone's dependence on the land was obvious, they made a very big thing of this four-day period.

On Monday, Tuesday, and Wednesday the main feature of the observance was a procession around the perimeter of the parish. This was known as "beating the bounds." With all the stops for prayers, sermons, blessings, picnics, and side trips to nearby pubs it could easily take three days to get all the way around some parishes. It was a serious and reverent matter, no question about that, but when you have a whole congregation on a three-day outing there will inevitably be some shenanigans. Some of the faithful managed to have a good deal of fun along the way.

144

We get our food from the supermarket shelves today, and it is hard to make ourselves aware of any hook-up with farms, flocks, and orchards. So on Rogation Sunday some clergymen take the occasion to preach about the labors of the husbandman and the fruits of the earth, but the three following days go pretty much unnoticed.

ROOD, ROOD SCREEN, ROOD BEAM.
See under CHANCEL SCREEN.

RUBRICS.
From the Latin *rubrica:* red. The Latin word itself goes back to an older word, *ruber,* which was the name of the red earth used as chalk by carpenters.

Rubrics are directions for the conduct of services. Some are for the clergy; some for the laity. They are printed at the beginning of each service and throughout the text, to tell the clergy and people what to do at each point as the service proceeds. The trouble is that hardly anyone reads them. Episcopalians would be much more sure of themselves in church if they took a little time to read the rubrics.

In most of the Prayer Books found in the pews the rubrics are printed in black italics. In the more expensive books used by the clergy they are in red, which is why they are called rubrics.

It was the custom of Roman jurists to use red for the titles under which they listed their laws. Finally they wrote the laws, too, in red. The practice of the lawyers was adopted by the Christian Church.

The word "rubric" has been taken over into popular language and now can be made to mean almost any rule or regulation, whether in or out of church.

SABBATARIANISM. In a general sense this word means excessive strictness in the observance of Sunday. In ecclesiastical terminology it refers to the official policy of certain Protestant denominations, all of which confuse Sunday with the Sabbath. See SABBATH.

The Puritans, for example, were Sabbatarians. When in 1644 they got control of Parliament, they passed a series of laws that prohibited just about everything on Sunday except attendance at religious services. No recreation at all was allowed; no playing of music or singing, no reading of anything but the Bible. One couldn't even go for a walk.

After the Stuarts were restored to the throne (1660) things were loosened up a bit. Recreation was again permitted. But a special Sunday mood had been created in England, and some of the old lugubrious flavor remained until quite recent times. In former colonies, for example Canada or Australia, things are still closed up pretty tightly on Sundays.

The strangest thing about this repression is that, although it was brought about by the English and Scottish Calvinists, it has no discernible connection with Calvinism. John Calvin himself was by no means a Sabbatarian, nor were any of the Calvinist churches on the European continent.

The Puritans in New England were as austere about Sunday observance as their relatives in the old country, and some of their influence is still visible in parts of the United States.

SABBATH. From the Hebrew *shabhath:* to rest.

The Jewish name for the seventh day of the week.

The fourth of the Ten Commandments (Exodus 20: 8-11) orders that this day be kept holy by complete abstinence from work. It represents the rest God took after he had spent six days making "heaven and earth, the sea, and all that is in them." See the story of Creation, Genesis 1: 1 to 2: 3.

The Sabbath, then, is Saturday, not Sunday as many suppose. And it is Jewish, not Christian. The early Christians kept it because they were Jews, but they very soon made Sunday their weekly holy day because both the resurrection and the coming of the Holy Spirit (Pentecost) had occurred on the first day of the week. For a while they observed both the Sabbath and Sunday. Later, as Christianity spread over the Gentile world, Jewish practices and customs faded out gradually, the Sabbath along with the others.

It is a mistake to say, as the Puritans did and some sects still do, that the Christian Church simply transferred the Sabbath to Sunday. The character of our Sunday observance is not at all the same as the Jewish requirements for the Sabbath. With the Jews the rule against work expanded into a lengthy set of regulations so detailed that no one could even remember them all, let alone obey them. For example, if you wanted to sit in the shade on the Sabbath you had to arrange several chairs beforehand, so that as the shade moved you could go from one chair to another. To carry the chair would be a violation of the Sabbath law.

Sunday is certainly not like that. It is a festival day. Every Sunday is a "little Easter." The Sunday morning prayer on page 595 of the Prayer Book begins, "O God, who makest us glad with the weekly remembrance of the glorious resurrection of thy Son our Lord." It is a glad day.

Because it is a glad day no Sunday can ever be a day

of gloomy restrictions. In Lent Sundays are exempted from the Lenten fast.

Sunday is, of course, a day of rest and worship—and recreation. It is a holy day, different from any other day of the week. But it is not the Sabbath.

SACRAMENT. From the Latin *sacrare:* to consecrate.

In the Roman civilization a *sacramentum* was an oath of allegiance, a consecrating of oneself to some cause or organization. St. Augustine said a Christian sacrament was "the visible form of an invisible grace"—something you can see that is outward evidence of an inner attitude you can't see. St. Augustine took a familiar secular word and used it as an illustration of the inevitable intermingling of spirit and matter. When someone stands up and holds up his right hand and pronounces the formal words of an oath —this is an outward action that shows how he feels inside. Everyone had been through that experience or had seen others go through it. Augustine's meaning was not hard to grasp.

We live in the kind of world where we have only material ways of expressing ourselves spiritually. In such a world much of life is necessarily sacramental in essence. Our relationships with one another are made and maintained by *things* we can see that reveal *deeper realities* we can't see.

A kiss, for example, is sacramental in nature. So is a handshake, or a gift. So, certainly, is what a man does with his money. There is no clearer public announcement of the condition of a man's soul than the way he uses his money. Material things and physical actions are the only tools the spirit has to work with. We are all acquainted with the sacramental principle. We live with it and by it.

In the church vocabulary a sacrament is defined as

"an outward and visible sign of an inward and spiritual grace given unto us; ordained by Christ himself, as a means whereby we receive this grace, and a pledge to assure us thereof."* This definition is obviously built on St. Augustine's earlier one.

* See Offices of Instruction, Book of Common Prayer, page 292.

There was no general agreement as to how many sacraments there are until about the eleventh century. By that time the number had pretty well settled to seven, but this was not made official until the Council of Trent, in the middle of the sixteenth century. The seven were: Baptism, Holy Communion, Confirmation, Penance, Holy Orders, Matrimony, and Extreme Unction.

At the Reformation the Reformers kept only Baptism and the Holy Communion, rejecting the other five for two reasons: (1) they are not of the Gospel, and (2) they carry no visible sign or ceremony ordained by God.*

Note: The consecrated host (the bread of the Holy Communion) is often called "the Sacrament," especially when it is "reserved," that is, kept in the church between services for the Communion of the sick and/or adoration.

See RESERVED SACRAMENT.

* See Article XXV in the Articles of Religion, back of Prayer Book.

SACRISTAN. A term now mostly replaced by the word "sexton."

In earlier times the sacristan was the man in charge of the sacristy, the room in which were kept the sacred vessels of the Holy Communion, the altar hangings, the priestly vestments, the candlesticks, etc. He was, more often than not, in holy orders.

About the only places where you now find a sacristan in the original sense is in cathedrals, some of which have ordained priests called Canon Sacristans.

SACRISTY. From the Latin *sacer:* sacred, set apart. The sacristy is a room adjoining a church or chapel in which the Eucharistic vessels, the altar hangings, and various ceremonial objects are kept. If there is enough space there are also cupboards for the clergy's vestments; if not, the vestments are hung in another room close by, called the vestry (q.v.).

SAINT. From the Latin *sanctus:* holy. In the original meaning of the word saints are just "holies"—holy persons.

By the Roman Catholic definition saints are (1) "all the inhabitants of heaven" and (2) "in the strict sense, those who have received the official approval of the Church for public veneration, this approval being given because of the holy and virtuous lives which these persons lived on earth, and because of the attestation of God by certified miracles obtained through their intercession."* This makes no allowance for living saints, of whom we know by experience that there are many, but it is in this "strict sense" that the word "saint" is now generally used, not only by Romanists but also by Anglicans and others.

* *The National Catholic Almanac* (American)—1954 edition.

It did not start out that way. St. Paul, believing, as the old hymn puts it, that Christ "died to make men holy," applied the term to all Christians. He wrote "to all that be in Rome, beloved of God, called to be saints," to "them that are sanctified in Christ Jesus, called to be saints" in Corinth, and "to the saints which are at Ephesus." To him everybody in the Church was a saint.

It was not long, however, before the designation

began to be reserved for the departed and limited to those who had been martyred for the faith or who had shown extraordinary holiness in their lives.

At first such persons were declared saints simply by local acclamation. A good man or woman in the Christian community died and everyone agreed, without formal debate, that he or she was a saint. All such a declaration needed to make it valid was the bishop's endorsement.

It is easy to see how this free-wheeling procedure would lead to an unmanageable proliferation of saints. Slowly the Church began to clamp down. Wider approval became necessary, first from a synod and finally, in the thirteenth century, from the Pope. The first saint canonized by a Pope was Ulrich, Bishop of Augsburg, in 993. The Pope was John XV.

It was two more centuries before Alexander decreed that the Pope and only the Pope should make the decision in all cases. It was not really necessary for him to issue this order. By this time all cases *were* being submitted to him. Alexander's decree became general law under Gregory IX in the thirteenth century.

The Roman machinery for canonization is slow, complex, and thorough. It involves two exhaustive investigations, first in the candidate's own diocese, and then, if he passes the diocesan tests, a second one in Rome. Probed at both levels are his biography, his writings, and the evidence of miracles worked through his intercession both before and after his death. In the diocese and again in Rome there is an opponent appointed who is known as "the devil's advocate." His job is to dig up anything he can find against the candidate.

If all goes well in the investigations the person is "beatified," that is, he is declared by the Pope to be residing in heaven because of his saintly life and heroic virtue. After beatification he or she is called "Blessed," as, for example, Blessed Oliver Plunkett or Blessed Lucy of Narni.

Once beatified, the candidate has a good chance of going on to sainthood. About all that is required in addition to what has already been determined about him is proof of two miracles attributable to him since his beatification.

The Eastern Orthodox Church is much less rigid than Rome about canonization. Its method is more like that followed in early times in the West. The bishop has authority to declare a certain person a saint by issuing a solemn proclamation. This means, as it did centuries ago in the Western church, that some saints are purely local. One diocese has no obligation to recognize another diocese's saints.

In 1964 General Convention authorized the use of a volume of Collects, Epistles, and Gospels prepared by the Church's Standing Liturgical Commission for days commemorative of a number of heroic figures not now carried in the Book of Common Prayer. If it does not make them saints, this is at least a formal recognition of these giants of the faith. No systematic process of canonization has as yet been proposed for the Episcopal Church.

The Church of England, in 1661, did in fact canonize King Charles I, who was beheaded by the Puritans under Cromwell in 1649. St. Charles the Martyr's day was set as January 30 (the day on which he died) and a whole day of commemorative services for him were put into the 1662 English Book of Common Prayer. For the Holy Communion there were two Collects (in one of which he was called a saint) and an Epistle and Gospel. Special prayers, Psalms, Scripture lessons, and Collects were also provided for Morning and Evening Prayer. There was no doubt of the Church's intention to declare Charles a saint. In

1859 Queen Victoria removed the services, after they had been there for 198 years. This was the only instance of "decanonizing" a saint anyone had ever heard of until Pope Paul VI began dropping them by the score in 1968.

With very few exceptions a saint's day is the day on which he died, that is, the day on which he entered God's heavenly kingdom, which was considered much more momentous than the day he was born on this earth.

SANCTUARY. From the Latin *sanctus:* holy. The part of the church where the altar is. The interior of a church is usually divided into three sections or areas: the nave (q.v.), the chancel (q.v.), and the sanctuary. The sanctuary is the area behind the altar rail, or in the case of a free-standing altar, the area enclosed by the rail.

Of course the whole church is consecrated and, logically, no one place in it can be any holier than another, but we all tend to think of the sanctuary as especially sacred.

Many Protestant denominations call the entire inside of the church the sanctuary. The only basis for this would seem to be that they do not have the three traditional architectural divisions in their churches and consequently have no one section to designate as the "holy of holies."

SANCTUARY LAMP. A lamp hanging before the altar. Three such lamps may be used, or sometimes even seven, but usually there is just one. A single lamp burning continuously indicates the presence of the Reserved Sacrament (q.v.).

SANCTUS. The hymn of adoration in the Eucharist beginning with the words "Holy, Holy,

Holy." It is found on page 77 of the Prayer Book and again on page 79. The second time is for the convenience of the priest, to save him from having to turn back a page in case a Proper Preface has been read after the Sursum Corda.

The source of this hymn is Isaiah 6: 1–3, and a form of it was used in Jewish worship long before the Christian era. Christians began to include it as early as the third century.

Sanctus is Latin for "holy."

SANCTUS BELL. The right name is sacring bell, but everyone calls it the sanctus bell, obviously because it is rung at the time of the Sanctus, the "Holy, Holy, Holy." This is a bell used in all Roman and many Episcopal churches. It may be rung at the elevation of the bread and wine in the Eucharist as well as at the Sanctus.

The purpose of this bell-ringing was in former times to focus the people's attention. In big, dark medieval churches the congregation could not always see what the priest was doing, and even if they could hear the Latin he was intoning they couldn't understand it. So bells were rung at these two points in the service and everyone was brought up to date on what was going on at the altar.

SEDILIA. A Latin word meaning seats. Applied especially to the seats inside the altar rail used by the clergy and acolytes.

SEE. From the Latin *sedes:* seat. When first used, this word referred only to the bishop's seat, which was the earliest of all symbols of episcopal authority. The seat was kept in the cathedral, and the town where the cathedral was located was called the bishop's see.

154

Now, in church vocabulary, see has become a synonym for the whole diocese.

SEMINARY. A general term for all theological colleges. Many such institutions do not have the word "seminary" in their official titles, but in the popular mind and in popular language they are seminaries just the same.

SEXTON. A corruption of "sacristan" (q.v.). A sexton is a church custodian who takes care of the church and other parish buildings.

SIGN OF THE CROSS, THE. A ceremonial gesture, also called "crossing oneself" or "blessing oneself," which consists of touching, in sequence, the forehead, chest, left shoulder, and right shoulder. This is done on a variety of occasions, both in private devotions and public services of worship. It is most frequently associated with the saying of the words "In the Name of the Father, and of the Son, and of the Holy Ghost."

The custom of making the sign of the cross on one's person began as early as the second century, but it was at first only a small cross on the forehead, made with the thumb or index finger during private prayers. By the fourth century Christians were making these little crosses on both forehead and chest during Mass, but it was not until the thirteenth century that the large cross as we now know it came into universal and official use. It was ordered by Pope Innocent III and was to be made with three fingers, which stood for the Holy Trinity. Now it is done with the whole hand.

Roman Catholics make the sign of the cross. Eastern Orthodox Christians do too, though they do it a little differently: they end up going from the right to the left shoulder.

Many Anglicans cross themselves; many do not. The only mention of this sign in the Prayer Book occurs at the top of page 280, in the service of Holy Baptism. The rubric directs that "the Minister shall make a Cross upon" the forehead of the child or person he has just baptized.

SPY WEDNESDAY. See under HOLY WEEK.

STEWARDSHIP. Steward comes from the Old English *stig:* house, plus *weard:* guard. The guardian of the house. Expanded later to mean the man who looked after the owner's whole estate.

When the Church talks about stewardship it is putting property into its right perspective theologically. It is saying God owns everything—all those material objects we are accustomed to call ours—and we are stewards whose job it is to take care of his property. Rightly understood, this belief can change a man's whole idea of why he is alive on this earth.

It is a shame when the money-raising boys get hold of so powerful a concept as stewardship and debase it into a way of increasing church income. They distort it into meaning "the more money you give to the church the better steward you are," which may not be true at all. God may have some other place where he wants that money used.

Anyway, stewardship is concerned not only with money. There are many things besides dollars and cents that you are holding in trust for God. You are supposed to use them all thoughtfully and responsibly. You can't be a good steward by just giving money to the church.

Properly taught, the idea of stewardship can become a means of grace. Used as a gimmick, it gives about as much nourishment to the soul as a campaign to buy new uniforms for the local high school band.

STALL. A special seat in the choir of a cathedral, assigned to an honored individual, usually a clergyman but sometimes some secular dignitary such as, in the British Isles, a Lord Mayor. The name or title of the occupant is lettered above the seat or on the back-rest of it.

The term is also applied in a general sense to the seats in the chancel of any church: for example, "choir stalls."

In ordinary speech we use the word in reference to the compartments in barns in which horses or other animals are kept, and the Old English word *stealle,* from which we get "stall," meant exactly that.

STANDING COMMITTEE. The Constitution of the Episcopal Church requires that every diocese have a Standing Committee, consisting of clergy and laity, appointed by the Diocesan Convention.

As long as the diocese has a bishop the Standing Committee's chief responsibility is to act as his council of advice, and he is under no obligation to take their advice.

But when the diocese is without a bishop the Standing Committee becomes the Eccesiastical Authority until a new bishop is enthroned. Of course this does not mean that the Standing Committee in the absense of a bishop has power to confirm or ordain. It means they do the paper work that normally falls to the bishop.

SUFFRAGAN BISHOP. See under BISHOP.

SURSUM CORDA. Latin for "Lift up your hearts." The four-line antiphon between priest and people, found on page 76 of the Prayer Book. It has been a part of the Eucharist since the third century.

SYNOD. From the Greek *sunodos:* a meeting. A synod, literally, could be any kind of meeting, but very early in Christian history it came to mean a gathering of clergy. After that it loosened up enough to include laymen, but it is still a meeting having to do with church business.

The only synods you will hear about in the Episcopal Church are those of our nine provinces (q.v.). The bishops and elected clerical and lay representatives of the dioceses in the province meet annually except in General Convention years (one or two provinces don't even skip those years) and take care of whatever business there is to come before the province, which usually isn't much.

These synods have no power, but they do make suggestions, sometimes some very good ones, to the General Convention, and as the Church grows and General Convention keeps on becoming more and more unwieldy, it would not be surprising if we were forced into some sort of reorganization that would give the synods more importance.

TABERNACLE. From the Latin *tabernaculum:* a tent. When the Church uses the word "tabernacle" it is referring to a box-like compartment on an altar that holds vessels containing the consecrated bread of the Sacrament, that is, the "Reserved Sacrament."

To call an intricately carved and sometimes richly ornamented box a tent may seem to be stretching the original word rather recklessly, but it isn't really. An altar tabernacle is usually lined with draped folds of white silk and its interior does have some resemblance to a tent.

The tabernacle first appeared on altars in the sixteenth century.

TE DEUM. The first two words of the Latin hymn *Te Deum laudamus*, ("We praise thee, O God"), an anthem in rhythmical prose. Tradition says it was composed spontaneously by St. Ambrose and St. Augustine on the occasion of St. Augustine's baptism. This theory of its origin is generally rejected now, and scholars, with some hesitation, attribute it to St. Niceta, who was Bishop of Romesiana (now part of Yugoslavia) in the fifth century.

The Te Deum is included in our service of Morning Prayer (Prayer Book, pages 10 and 11) and is quite regularly used in parish churches, especially on festival days.

Many composers—Handel was one—have written elaborate musical settings for the Te Deum, and these are often used apart from Morning Prayer on occasions of great joy or thanksgiving.

TENTMAKING MINISTRY. A whimsical, semi-poetical way of describing the ministry of clergymen who make their livings in secular professions or trades and don't get any pay for what they do as clergymen. The term refers to St. Paul's practice of supporting himself—according to tradition he made tents—while he was going about the Roman Empire preaching the Gospel.

The tentmakers of our time are the business and professional men who have been ordained and who help out, mostly but not only in their own parishes, thus augmenting the clerical staff at little or no expense to the congregation.

THANKSGIVING OF WOMEN AFTER CHILDBIRTH, THE. Commonly called the Churching of Women. See The Book of Common Prayer, pages 305-307.

The thanksgiving in this service is for a safe delivery rather than for the child.

The rite is a vestigial survival of the Jewish ceremony of purification, which took place forty days after the birth of a male child, eighty days in the case of a female. During that period the new mother was considered ritually "unclean." To us the term "unclean" sounds harsh and unjust. It seems to imply that there is moral defilement in the reproductive process.

The real rationale of it is that following the birth of a child it takes about six weeks, more or less, for the mother's pelvic organs to heal and to regain their natural elasticity. During this time the birth canal is unusually liable to infection or even perforation. Doctors advise women to refrain from sexual intercourse until after their first post-partum check-up, which, varying according to the individual doctor's rule, occurs from four to six weeks after delivery. The Jews, intensely religious, protected the woman by an ecclesiastical tabu. Our secularly orientated culture makes her protection a medical matter. Both approaches have the same purpose: to assure the woman an undisturbed time for recuperation.

For many years the early Christians, being mostly Jews at first, carried on the Jewish purification rite in the form to which they were accustomed. As an act of thanksgiving only, the service is first mentioned late in the sixth century, though it must have been on the way to acquiring this character for some time previous to that. The 1549 Book of Common Prayer (Anglicanism's first one) shows that the purification idea had not even at that late date wholly disappeared. The service there is titled "The Purification of Women," although the content is entirely an expression of gratitude, with no hint of any need of cleansing. In the 1552 revision the title is changed to the one we still use: "The Thanks Geuing of Women after Childe Birth."

The Churching of Women is not an obligatory service in the Anglican or any other church. It has never become popular in America, partly, one supposes, because of the Puritan mood of this country's early days, and perhaps partly because of Victorian shyness about such matters.

THIRTY-NINE ARTICLES, THE. A set of doctrinal formulae beginning on page 603 of the Prayer Book. Their proper title is "Articles of Religion," but they are usually called the Thirty-nine Articles, just because there are thirty-nine of them.

The first thing you have to know about them in order to understand them is that they were written in an attempt to hold the Church of England together when it was being pulled in all directions by Romanists, Puritans, Lutherans, and traditional Anglicans. This was during the reign of Elizabeth I, and even the Queen herself took a hand in composing them.

They are therefore not so much statements of Anglican doctrine as efforts to deal with specific disputed points without alienating any of the disputing parties. The result was that some of them are masterpieces of ambiguity and some lean over backward trying to avoid taking any side at all.

After a number of bishops and other theologians had tugged and strained at them for twenty years, an impatient Parliament stepped in, in 1571, and made them the law of the land in just about the form they now have. From that time on until 1865 all English clergymen were required to subscribe to them. Since 1865 the clergy have had only to say the Articles are agreeable to the Word of God and promise not to teach anything in contradiction of them.

The Articles were not put into the American Prayer Book until 1801, and the American clergy have never been asked to subscribe to them. Because they are part of the Prayer Book it is considered enough that the clergyman before his ordination takes an oath to conform to the doctrine, discipline, and worship of the Church. A separate oath about the Articles would be redundant.

In any consideration of the Articles of Religion it must be remembered that our doctrine is covered by the Prayer Book as a whole. The Articles are to be interpreted in the light of the Prayer Book, not the other way around.

Laymen, in America or England, have never been required to subscribe to the Articles.

THURIBLE. From the Latin *thus:* incense. A metal vessel in which incense is burned at religious ceremonies. Usually it is suspended on chains, from which it can be swung. It is also called a "censer."

THURIFER. The person who carries the thurible (q.v.) at religious ceremonies.

TITHE. An Old English word meaning "tenth." The Jews were commanded (Deuteronomy 14: 22) to "truly tithe all the increase of thy seed." For convenience they were permitted to convert the seed into money and pay a tenth in currency. Since Church and State were then one, their tithe covered both taxes and offering. Logically, by this criterion, we all tithe, and more, when we pay our income tax, but if we took this position the Church would get no money at all and none of us wants it that way.

The "modern tithe," vigorously urged in many parts of the Church today, suggests that over and above our taxes we set aside ten per cent of our income (here there is some legalistic quibbling about whether it should be gross or net income) for church and charity. Five per cent for each is the recommended division.

Certainly this ten per cent goal has by no means been achieved nationwide, but the promotion of it across the country has greatly increased the Church's income in the last twenty-five years.

TONGUES, SPEAKING IN. See GLOS-SALALIA.

TRANSEPT. From the Latin *trans:* across, and *septum:* a partition. Either of the two lateral arms of a cruciform church (q.v.).

TRANSUBSTANTIATION. From the Latin *trans:* change, and *substantia:* substance. Theologically it has to do with the bread and wine in the Holy Communion and it means exactly what these two Latin words say: a change of substance.

Transubstantiation is the dogma that holds that the substance of the bread and wine, when consecrated by a priest, change into the substance of the Body and Blood of Christ, with only the "appearance" of the bread and wine remaining. It takes literally the Lord's statement at the Last Supper: "This is my body" and "This is my blood." (Matthew 26: 26 and 28, and other passages in the Gospels and the Epistles.) Belief in this actual physical change was declared to be necessary to salvation by the Lateran Council in 1215.

We Anglicans are not required to accept it. Some do; most don't.

See REAL PRESENCE.

TRINITY, THE HOLY. From the Latin *trinitas:* a triad, or union of three. In Christian theology the dogma that God exists in three Persons (Father, Son, and Holy Spirit) yet is not three gods but one entity in substance or essence.

To the laymen, and for that matter to many clergymen, there is no more baffling, obscure, incomprehensible statement in the whole system of Christian doctrine. There never has been an acceptable definition of the Trinity and there probably never will be one. It just won't come into words.

The Bible is no help. St. Paul says (II Corinthians 13: 14), "the grace of the Lord Jesus Christ and the love of God and the fellowship of the Holy Spirit be with you," and St. Matthew 28: 19 quotes Jesus as saying, "Go therefore and make disciples of all nations, baptizing them in the name of the Father and of the Son and of the Holy Spirit." The Persons are named, but nowhere does the New Testament even mention the word "trinity," let alone present it as a dogma.

We can get a working idea of what it is about if we think of it as describing the three ways God relates himself to us. The Catechism (Prayer Book, page 578) says we "believe in God the Father, who hath made me, and all the world, in God the Son, who hath redeemed me, and all mankind, (and) in God the Holy Ghost, who sanctifieth me, and all the people of God." In other words, we know God as the architect and builder of all Creation; we know him as the man who spent thirty years on this earth in human form and loved us so much that he came back even after we killed him; and we know him as the Spirit that lives in our hearts, strengthening us and propelling us toward holiness.

This is by no means a definition of the doctrine of the Trinity, but it may be of practical help to some who are trying to understand what the theologians are trying to say.

U and V

UNCTION. From the Latin *unguere:* to anoint. In Christian practice unction is the process of anointing with consecrated oil for some religious reason. Episcopalians apply the term almost exclusively to the anointing of sick persons for the purpose of making them well. It is beyond any doubt that this healing ceremony has been performed since earliest Christian times. It is referred to in the New Testament in Mark 6: 13 and James 5: 14.

The first English Prayer Book, published in 1549, contained a service of unction, in which there was a prayer for the healing of body and mind, for forgiveness, and for spiritual strengthening. This service has not appeared in any subsequent edition of the English Prayer Book.

A brief ceremony called Unction of the Sick was introduced into our American Prayer Book in 1928 (page 320) at the conclusion of the Order for the Visitation of the Sick, which begins on page 308. The rubric accompanying it directs that unction be used together with such parts of the service as the minister "shall think fit." This rubric also says it shall be administered "when any sick person shall in humble faith desire" it, which would seem to indicate that the initiative lies with the patient.

The power of healing was given to the Apostles (Matthew 10: 1 and Luke 9: 1), which appears to make it a priestly function, and it has generally been so regarded by the Church. Our rubric is therefore confusing, since it uses the word "minister," not "priest." If oil is used this wording does not really present any difficulty, since it is always oil that has been blessed by the bishop, and the Apostolic Ministry is thus represented. But our service permits the laying on of hands as an alternative to anointing, and the term "minister" implies that the hands need not be priestly ones. The Prayer Book is always quite specific in its language about actions that are limited to the priesthood.

VEIL. From the Latin *vela:* a sail or a curtain. A veil, as everyone knows, is a piece of cloth, usually flimsy and transparent so that the wearer may be able to see through it. But when we talk about veils in church we mean either:

(1) the solid cloth that covers the chalice at the Eucharist, or
(2) the loose-woven netting that is draped over all crosses, crucifixes, and pictures in the church during Passiontide. These veils are usually violet in color except on Maundy Thursday, when white is used.

VERGER. A term not much used in America. Literally, a verger is the official who carries a mace, or "verge" (from the Latin *verga:* a rod) before some dignitary at formal affairs. The dignitary need not be an ecclesiastical personage—the Lord Mayor, for example, might be preceded by a verger with a mace.

166

Today the word has come to mean in England just about what "sexton" means in this country, that is, one who takes care of the church and other parish buildings.

VESTMENTS. From the Latin *vestis:* garment. In the literal, original sense, therefore, anything you put on is a vestment. For our purpose here, vestments are the distinctive items of dress worn by the clergy when they are conducting services of public worship.

Some vestments, over the centuries, have acquired a massive amount of symbolism, but this is all medieval and modern accretion. The fact is that everything a clergyman wears now started out with no ecclesiastical significance whatever. In the early days he dressed like everyone else in the Roman Empire. Even at the altar he wore the familiar everyday clothes of the people: a tunic, and perhaps a toga over it.

Between the sixth and ninth centuries secular fashions began to change. The trend was toward making a man's clothes a sign of his trade or profession, so that it became possible to tell a grocer or a bricklayer or a doctor by the way he was dressed. The Church adjusted to this fashion by the simple means of *not* adjusting to it. The clergy just went on wearing what they had always worn: the now obsolete garb of earlier generations. Their stated reason was that these had been the clothes of the saints and martyrs and they didn't want to give them up. The result was that they achieved their identifying garb by merely staying old-fashioned.

As time went on the clergy's clothes became stylized; they gathered an encrustation of invented meanings; and as secular clothes became more elegant the vestments grew more ornate too. They began to be made of rich materials, such as silk and velvet, and to be decorated with embroidery and tassels and sometimes even jewels.

Here is a list of the vestments worn today, together with the meanings some of them have accumulated through the years.

FOR MORNING AND EVENING PRAYER

Morning and Evening Prayer are often called the "choir offices" because they are said in the chancel, or choir, of the church rather than at the altar. Proper dress for the clergyman at these services are the following garments:

The cassock. From the Persian *kazhaghand:* a padded jacket. A loose-fitting robe reaching to the floor, worn under the surplice or the Eucharistic vestments (see below). It may be of any color but is ordinarily black. There are two styles of cassock: the Roman, which buttons all the way down the front, and the Anglican, double or single-breasted, which has no buttons except at the neck, and is held in place at the waist by a cloth band or a buckled belt. Lovers of symbolism say this waist band signifies self-control. Originally the cassock was a secular coat worn by both men and women. Down to the beginning of the nineteenth century, long after it had gone out of style among the general populace, it was the customary outdoor dress of the clergy in England. It still is in some countries.

It is also worn in church by choristers and acolytes under their surplices, and by vergers (q.v.) as an outer garment.

The clerical vest is clearly a shortened form of the cassock, made to be worn with jacket and trousers.

The surplice. From the Latin *super:* over, plus *pellicum:* fur coat. (The derivation indicates the necessary undergarments once worn by clergy in unheated churches.) The white garment worn over the cassock. The ones in common use today are much shorter than those worn before the Reformation, which fell well below the knee. The surplice is put on over the head, and in the days when parsons, like everyone else, wore wigs, it had a slit down the front, fastened by a button at the neck, so that the wearer might not disturb his coiffure. Some surplices are trimmed with, or made entirely of, lace, but this is not usual in the Anglican Church.

The cotta. From Old High German *kozza:* a coarse mantle. A still shorter form of the surplice. Worn more by acolytes and choristers than by clergy.

The tippet. Derived by some obscure evolution from the Middle English word *tipet,* which meant "point." The modern tippet could hardly be described as a point. It is a black scarf that hangs around the neck and down the front. For those who hold a master's or a doctor's degree the tippet is made of silk; for bachelors and non-graduates it is made of a woolen cloth the British call "stuff." In the choir offices it is the only vestment that distinguishes the clergyman from the choristers. It is also referred to as a "scarf."

The hood. From the Anglo-Saxon *hod:* a flexible covering for the head. The kind of hood we are talking about here, however, is no longer worn over the head, but around the neck and down the back. It is an academic insignia showing what kind of college degree the wearer holds. There are three kinds of degree: doctor's, master's, and bachelor's. Which of the three the hood represents is shown by its length and by the width of the velvet band that runs about its edge. The color of the velvet band indicates the field of study in which the degree was attained. Most clergymen's hoods have a red band, for red is the color for a degree in divinity. The colors of the hood's silk lining are those of the college that awarded the degree.

FOR THE HOLY COMMUNION
Vestments worn by the celebrant (q.v.) at the Holy Communion are called Eucharistic vestments. Eucharist is one of several names for this sacrament.

THE VESTMENTS ARE:
The amice. From the Latin *amicire:* to wrap around. A collar of white linen worn over the cassock. It was originally nothing more than a kerchief, but by the ninth century people were saying it stood for "the helmet of salvation" and the priest was resting it on the top of his head for a few moments before putting it into its proper position around his neck.

The alb. From the Latin *albus:* white. A long white linen robe reaching down to the hem of the cassock. It has straight sleeves. It is put on over the head, as a surplice is. The alb is said to be the oldest Christian vestment. A more accurate way of putting it would be to say that it goes back to times when it was not a Christian vestment at all but an article of everyday dress for the whole populace.

The alb is explained as representing the white robe our Lord wore. There can be little doubt that he did wear such a robe, but so did almost everyone else.

The girdle. From the Old English *gyrdan:* something that encircles. This is a linen rope or a band of cloth worn, of course, about the waist. Its utilitarian purpose is obvious. Symbolists, however, can't let it go at that. They say the girdle is a reminder that our Lord was bound by a rope. Also called a cincture.

The stole. From the Greek *stole:* raiment. This silk band, worn about the neck and hanging down in front, is the essential insignia of the ordained ministry. Only bishops, priests, and deacons are permitted to wear it. (A deacon wears a stole over his left shoulder and loosely tied on his right side.)

When used in the Holy Communion service the stole follows the seasonal colors; in other sacraments its color varies according to the occasion. At the Eucharist it is crossed in front, right over left, and held in place by loops in the girdle. A bishop wears the stole uncrossed.

Here again symbolism has been brought in. The stole is said to be the yoke of obedience to Christ.

The maniple. From the Latin *manus:* hand. In the early days of Christianity this vestment was probably only a kerchief or napkin carried over the arm by everybody as standard equipment. Apparently many centuries went by before some genius invented pockets. The maniple has become formalized into a narrow strip of silk or linen, usually in the seasonal color, worn over the celebrant's left arm just above the wrist.

Those who have to find a sacred meaning for all the vestments say the maniple represents the shackles with which our Lord's hands were bound.

The chasuble. From the Latin *casula:* a cloak. This is the outermost of all the Eucharistic vestments. It is oval in shape, with an opening in the center for the head, so that when worn it is the same shape seen from either front or back. The chasuble may be of silk or brocade in the color of the season, or it may be of plain white linen. Colored chasubles are sometimes richly adorned with gold embroidery and even jewels. The decorations are on Y-shaped strips called "or- phreys," usually only on the back of the garment but sometimes also on the front. The upper points of the Y run up to the shoulders; the base goes down from the intersection to the bottom edge of the chasuble.

The chasuble was originally an outer coat issued to Roman soldiers in cold weather. Symbolists say it rep- resents our Lord's "coat without seam" (John 19: 23), for which the soldiers at the cross cast lots.

The cope. From the Latin *capa:* a head covering. A strange name for an ornate, silk cloak which if laid out flat would be semicircular in shape and when worn hangs to the floor. It is open in front, held together by a clasp at the top. A vestige of the hood from which it gets its name is the shield-shaped piece of embroidery at the back of the neck, where a hood would be if there were one.

In America copes are most often worn by bishops, but there is no reason why any clergyman cannot wear one. In England the cope is standard equipment in many parish churches. They are still considered a lit- tle "high church" here in this country, though they are coming more and more into use.

THE BISHOP'S VESTMENTS

Bishops and cathedral clergy wear purple cassocks—the bishops as a badge of their elevated rank, the cathedral clergy to show they are on the staff of the bishop's church. Purple is probably the earliest successful dye known. It was taken from a shellfish called "purpura." It was very expensive and, because only the rich could afford it, purple clothing im- mediately became the mark of the carriage trade, the emblem of high position.

Besides the cassock bishops wear some of the vestments listed above, namely the stole, the tippet, the hood, and the cope. But these are also worn by clergy of lesser status. Vestments belonging exclusively to the bishop's office are:

The rochet. Probably of Germanic origin, from *roc:* coat. It is a white linen vestment much like the alb except that it has large sleeves, puffed at the shoulders and gathered at the wrists by silk bands, red or black. From time to time these ample sleeves, with their fluted cuffs turn up briefly in women's fashions, called, appropriately, "bishop's sleeves."
The rochet goes on over the cassock.

The chimere. Probably from Middle Latin *chimera:* a loose sleeveless garment. The chimere is the bishop's outer garment if he is not wearing a cope. It is made of silk or satin and may be either black or red.

The mitre. From the Greek *mitra:* a headband. This official headdress for bishops has gone through a good deal of evolution since it started out as a cone-shaped cap, much like a dunce cap. About 1100 it was changed to a plain round cap, made of soft, padded material. When they began to decorate it with an embroidered band running from front to back over the top, the band caused the soft cloth to bulge on either side. Next, these bulges were exaggerated into points and the mitre became a two-pointed headgear. The final step was to give the hat a quarter-turn so that the points were in the front and back instead of on the sides. And this, with two tabs of ribbon, called "lappets," hanging a few inches down the back, is the modern mitre.

After all that step-by-step development, there are those who say the mitre represents the "cloven tongues of fire" (a symbol of the Holy Spirit) that appeared over the heads of the Apostles on Pentecost. One wonders what they said it represented when it looked like a dunce cap.

The following items are not vestments, but they are also part of the bishop's equipment:

The pectoral cross. "Pectoral" is from the Latin *pectoris:* chest, or breast.

The pectoral cross may be a lavish thing of gold and precious stones, or it may be a plain silver cross. It is worn on a chain about the neck and hangs to the chest, hence its name. Of course, no one can stop any clergyman from wearing a cross on a chain around his neck if he wants to, and a great many of the "inferior clergy" do wear them. But the crosses they wear are usually small and very simple and are not likely to be confused with the bishop's imposing pectoral cross.

The ring. Bishops did not wear rings for several centuries after the Church began. There was no practical reason for them and the early Christians were not given to finery for its own sake. But gradually bishops became men of importance, controlling a considerable amount of property and engaging in a variety of legal actions that needed to be attested by an authoritative seal. So the bishop began to need a signet ring.

It is still simply a signet ring, a seal with which to mark official papers. It is worn by the bishop at all times.

The crozier. From Old High German *krucka:* crutch. A staff, often of silver, made in the form of a shepherd's crook, symbolizing the bishop's role as head of his "flock."

For an archbishop the crozier is a cross rather than a shepherd's crook.

There are no directions about vestments in the canons or in the Book of Common Prayer. In the latter, only in the second rubric on the Form and Manner for Ordering Priests, page 536, is anything even remotely related to the subject mentioned, and all the rubric says is that those who are to be ordained must be "decently habited," which one would think ought to apply to everyone present.

There just isn't any standard national rule. All is by custom and tradition, and all is pretty much local. Even neighboring parishes don't do everything the same way. So don't be embarrassed if you find yourself out of step in a strange church. Their customs are different from the ones you are used to, but that doesn't mean theirs are right and yours are wrong.

VESTRY. From the Latin *vestire:* to clothe or to put on. In church parlance the word has two meanings, the first now almost completely overshadowed by the second. First it referred only to the room near the altar where the vestments are kept. This room is still called the vestry. But the secondary and derived meaning of vestry now is that group of laymen (wardens and vestrymen) who are charged with the responsibility for the material affairs of the parish. When such a group first came into being, in the late Middle Ages, they held their meetings in the vestment room. That is how they came to be called the vestry.

Vestries as we know them are a peculiarly American institution. The early Church, having no property and no income, did not need such officers. When there began to be money and fabric to be looked after, the clergy handled it themselves at first and the laity had no say in these matters.

When wardens and sidesmen did appear in the parish organization they were not much like our American vestrymen. The warden's job was to keep the nave in repair. Note that his duties did not take him into the chancel or sanctuary—these parts of the church were too holy for a mere layman. The sidesman's task was to report at synods, under oath, on the moral condition of the parish from which he came.

When the American colonies won their independence and American Anglicans were faced with the task of writing a new Constitution and new Canons for their new Church, the vestry's rights and duties should have been defined at once in the light of the new situation. It sounds incredible, but it was not until 1877, a full century after the Revolution, that the American Church got around even to considering the question. They appointed a commission. At the General Convention of 1880 the commission reported no progress. The same thing happened every three years at General Convention until 1904, when the present Title I, Canon 13 was adopted. For a century-and-a-quarter vestrymen in this country did not know what their job was.

Canon 13 didn't help much. It says: (1) that "the number, mode of election, and term of office of Wardens and Vestrymen, with the qualifications of the voters, shall be such as the State or Diocesan law may permit or require," (2) "Except as provided by the law of the State or of the Diocese, the Vestry shall be agents and legal representatives of the Parish in all matters concerning its property and the relations of the Parish to its Clergy," and (3) "Unless it conflict with the law as aforesaid, the Rector, when present, shall preside in all the meetings of the Vestry." This boils down to just about nothing. The vestry has the authority to look after the business of the parish and straighten out troubles between the clergy and the congregation *IF the laws of the state and the diocese will let it.* So we have a national canon that doesn't really say anything.

Remember, though, that in 1904, when the canon

was written, the separation between Church and State was not nearly so complete as it is now. There were many old laws on the books then that have since been removed, and no state is likely today to interfere in church affairs. The diocese, of course, has a perfect right to add amplifications, details, and interpretations to national canons, and it is in diocesan canons that we find most of our regulations pertaining to vestries.

See WARDENS.

VICAR. From the Latin *vicarius:* a substitute.

In America a vicar is the priest in charge of a "mission," that is, a congregation financed wholly or in part by the diocese. Technically, the bishop is rector of all missions and the man who is actually on the premises, working in place of the bishop, is the bishop's substitute, or vicar.

VICARAGE. The house occupied by a vicar (q.v.) as his home, The vicarage is usually supplied by the diocese or by the mission to which the vicar ministers.

VIRGIN BIRTH. The doctrine that Mary conceived Jesus without having had sexual intercourse.

It has been said that religion is what you believe and theology is the way you try to say it. This aphorism is helpful in dealing with a doctrine that has been, especially in our scientific age, a stumbling-block to many who could accept all other Christian teachings but just couldn't get past this one, and didn't see any point to it anyway.

What the Church believes is not primarily concerned with how Mary received the necessary sperm but rather with the uniqueness of the child she bore. The Church believes that he was not just the most felicitous combination of human genes that ever fortuitously came together. He was both God and man.

177

His birth was beyond scientific law, for there is no scientific data regarding the birth of God in human form. It happened only once.

The theology, the attempt to put the belief into words, is the simple statement that he was born without a human father.

The purpose of the above explanation is only to clarify what the doctrine is saying on its deepest level. It is not intended either to argue for it or to "explain it away."

VISITATION. An official appearance by a diocesan bishop in one of his parishes.

The canon, "Of Duties of Bishops," says, "Every Bishop shall visit the Congregations within his jurisdiction at least once in three years," and it tells what he is to do on these visits. He goes there, the canon states:

    (1) To examine the condition of the parish. Whether this means the spiritual condition or the condition of the material fabric is not specified.

    (2) To inspect the behavior of the clergy.

    (3) To administer Confirmation.

    (4) To preach the Word.

    (5) At his discretion, to celebrate the Lord's Supper.

    (6) To examine the parish records.

W, X, Y, & Z

WARDENS. If you want to know what wardens do, you will have to look further than the national canons for most of your information.

Wardens are mentioned there only three times. The first time is in Title I, Canon 13, Sec. 1, which simply takes for granted that wardens and vestrymen exist in every parish and goes on to say that they shall be elected as the state or diocesan laws require and that they shall hold office until their successors are qualified. It does not even say that one is the senior and the other the junior warden.

The second allusion to wardens is in Title III, Canon 20, Sec. 5(a), which includes them in the list of persons who may certify to the Ecclesiastical Authority of the diocese that a local clergyman is not performing his duties.

Thirdly, Title III, Canon 22, Sec. 1, says, "the Churchwardens or other proper officers" shall let the bishop know when the parish becomes vacant.

And that is absolutely all the national Church has to say about wardens. Nowhere does it establish the office. It just assumes it.

Diocesan canons take it from there. Every diocese has its canons about wardens and vestrymen, and it is on this level that you have to look to find out what wardens are for.

In England there are two wardens, just as here in the United States. They are called respectively the Rector's Warden and the People's Warden. In America the English terminology was for some reason replaced with that of the Masonic Lodge and the wardens were called Senior and Junior.

These American terms are in no way helpful in describing the wardens' functions. The English designations do carry a hint of the job descriptions. At least they suggest that one warden represents the clergyman and the other represents the congregation in matters of communication and relationships. Many American parishes have gone back to the English titles, as being both more traditional and more descriptive.

It is an unfortunate fact that no general dictionary can tell much about wardens. Get a copy of your diocesan canons. That's where the details are.

WEDDING RING. The origin of the wedding ring was in the betrothal rings that were exchanged, before witnesses, by Roman couples when they announced their engagement. Christians adopted the custom at an early date. See under BETROTHAL.

The use of the fourth finger as the "ring finger" is thought to have come about through the introduction of the custom, now long discontinued, of saying the names of the Persons of the Trinity over the thumb, index finger, and middle finger as the ring was given. The fourth finger was reached as the groom said the Amen, and that is where the ring stopped and the marriage was sealed.

WHITSUNDAY OR PENTECOST. This is the day described in Acts 2: 1–4, when the Holy Ghost descended on the Apostles, as Jesus had promised them only a few days before, empowering them for the task ahead of them. It is considered the birthday of the Christian Church and in earlier times ranked second only to Easter as a festival. The day of Pentecost marks the end of the fifty-day celebration of Eastertide.

The Christian festival is called Pentecost because the event it commemorates took place on the Jewish day of Pentecost. The word "Pentecost" is not Jewish, though; it's Greek. It means "fiftieth." The Jews called the day the Feast of Weeks. It was the occasion, fifty days after Passover, when the first-fruits of the new grain crop were offered in gratitude for the harvest.

Why Anglicans have traditionally called it Whitsunday is open to some argument. It is always a

Sunday—that part is not debatable. But what does "whit" mean?

Some say it means "white," that the day is really White Sunday. Pentecost was always a big day for baptisms, second only to Holy Saturday, and the candidates for the sacrament all presented themselves in white robes. This theory is generally accepted.

But there are others who claim it comes from the Old English *wit* which can be translated "spirit." "Spirit Sunday"—an attractive idea, but it doesn't have the support of etymological scholars.

X. The common abbreviation for the Greek *Xristos:* Christ. From it we get Xmas for Christmas, Xn for Christian, Xy for Christianity. These short forms are handy for seminarians and scholars making notes, but in ordinary writing they are considered in questionable taste and by some are thought to be slightly irreverent.

YEAR, THE CHURCH. The Christian year is framed to emphasize the three greatest Christian feasts: Christmas, Easter, and Pentecost.

Christmas, having the fixed date of December 25, determines the date of the beginning of Advent, which is always the fourth Sunday before Christmas. (Epiphany, too, although it always falls on January 6, is in a sense dependent on Christmas. The reason it comes on January 6 is that the day is the first day after the end of the twelve-day Christmas season. If Christmas were not on December 25, Epiphany would not be on January 6.)

Easter, a movable feast, governs much of the Christian year. The length of the Epiphany season, and the dates of Ash Wednesday, Holy Week, Ascension Day,

Pentecost, and Trinity Sunday are all in relation to the date of Easter each year.

Pentecost, also called Whitsunday, the third great feast, falls fifty days after Easter. The purpose of the whole section of the year from Advent to Pentecost is to provide an annual review of the life of our Lord, from his birth to his sending of the Holy Spirit.

There are nine Church seasons. In order of their appearance they are: Advent, Christmas, Epiphany, Pre-Lent, Lent, Easter, Ascensiontide, Whitsuntide, and Trinity.

Besides Christmas there are the following immovable feasts: The Circumcision, January 1; The Purification of the Blessed Virgin Mary, February 2; The Annunciation of the Blessed Virgin Mary, March 25; and the Transfiguration of Christ, August 6. Also throughout the year are the saints' days, each with its own fixed date.

See all these festivals under their separate alphabetical listings.

YULE. A Scandinavian word, of which the literal meaning is "noise" or "clamor." Its chief association in ancient times was with the boisterous revelry that went along with the winter solstice festival.

Yule has nothing whatever to do with Christmas, but because the Christian celebration came at the same time of year English Christians, with their Teutonic background, just naturally held on to the word even though they had given up the pagan spree it described. They also kept some of the less riotous customs of the pagan Yuletide, such as the Yule log, for example.

ZION. Or Sion. A hill on the eastern ridge of the city of Jerusalem, taken by David from the Jebusites.

(II Samuel 5: 6 and 7). It became the seat of government of the kingdom of Israel.

The Jews considered this hill to be the earthly abode of God. Because of all the allusions to the holiness of Zion, many people have assumed that it must have been the site of Solomon's Temple. It wasn't. The Temple was north of Zion.

In the writings of Psalmists and prophets the word and its connotations of sanctity expanded to include the entire city of Jerusalem and finally all Israel. It is in this wider sense that the term "Zionism" is used to mean the establishment of a Jewish nation in Palestine. Going back to Zion is going back to the whole land, not just to a hill in Jerusalem.